P9-APN-992

sustainable architecture

hightechhousing

Concept: Arian Mostaedi
Publishers: Carles Broto & Josep Mª Minguet

Architectural Adviser: Pilar Chueca
Text: Contributed by the architects
Production & Graphic Design: Héctor Navarro

ISBN: 84-89861-79-X
D.L.: B-B-7162-2003

Printed in Spain

sustainable *architecture*

hightech**housing**

Index

Introduction

For all its merits, modern architecture has nonetheless been characterized, for far too long, by a general lack of ecological awareness. As the art that creates living space, thus establishing humankind's relationship with the environment, architecture should be one of the disciplines in which the ecological spirit reaches its maximum expression. However, this has not been the case. Until now.

If the new and ever-expanding field of sustainable architecture could be summed up in a few brief words, they might be, "with, not against". That is, rather than fighting the elements and our natural surroundings by installing cumbersome and inefficient heating and cooling systems, many architects are looking into ways to harness the energy in the natural elements, such as the sun, wind or earth, for creating self-sufficient energy systems. Furthermore, housing units are being designed which the occupants can adjust –opening or closing, ventilating or sealing off– according to the season or prevailing weather conditions. Finally, practices such as the use of ecological or recycled materials, or even simply using traditional materials more efficiently and wisely, are gaining ground.

Many of these ideas have been brought to life in the wide and varied selection of projects found on the following pages – work by such masters as Jean Nouvel, Helin & Sitonen, Norman Foster, and others.

Koh Kitayama + architecture WORKSHOP
Omni Quarter
Tokyo, Japan

This multi-purpose building, which is located in one of Tokyo's most sophisticated areas, has a basement floor, which houses an atelier, and four stories, covering a total floor area of 863m². Living quarters are on the third and fourth floors; a shop occupies the first and second floors.

A spacious, atrium-like space has been annexed onto the south side. This space serves the dual purpose of providing a stairwell which does not obstruct the central living space and an air layer that is part of a double-skin environmental control device.

This latter function is part of the architects' philosophy of designing structures which handle environmental conditions in a more rational manner: it is the inhabitants who decide when their home needs a "change of clothes", opening and closing household fixtures in response to the given climate and season.

This building also displays a characteristic which is not only typical of this studio's work, but to Asian house architecture in general: a planar format, with hallways and stairways placed at the periphery of the living area, thereby creating spaces which are easily adaptable to changes in daily living.

The building is an equal span rigid-frame structure with support columns on the inside, which frees up space in the hallways.

PHOTOGRAPHS: NOBUAKI NAKAGAWA

Site plan

The south-facing facade is an open air duct structure with slits. This space serves the dual purpose of providing a stairwell, which does not obstruct the central living space, and an air layer that is part of a double-skin environmental control device.

Feeling that Japanese architecture has tended in the past several years toward sterile and homogenous spaces, this studio sought a more "user-friendly" design. All skylights and openings can be opened or closed according to the season or weather conditions.

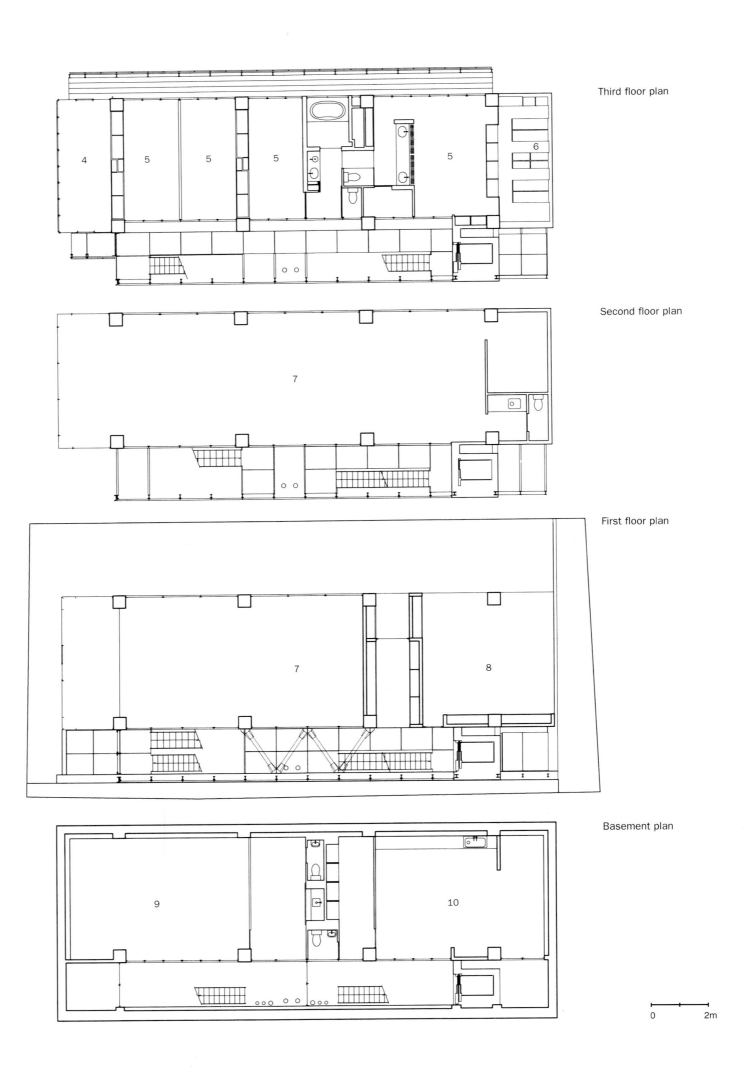

Third floor plan

Second floor plan

First floor plan

Basement plan

0   2m

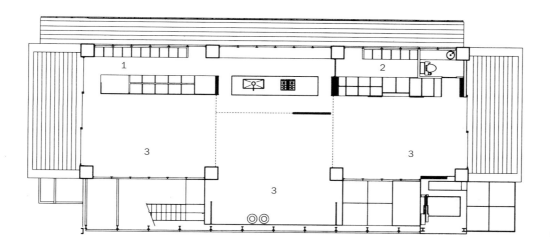

Fourth floor plan

1. Work space
2. Pantry
3. Multi-use room
4. Atelier
5. Private room
6. Cloak
7. Tenant
8. Parking area
9. Gallery
10. Ceramics atelier

Sir Norman Foster & Partners
Private House
Germany

This is a house for a young family with small children. The building is sited on a south-facing slope, which is well wooded and enjoys fine views to the valley beyond. The access road leads directly onto the roof terrace of the house, which is a two-story concrete and brickwork structure dug into the hillside. From this level, an entrance ramp leads down through the levels of the house to the lower garden terrace.

Both of these outdoor spaces are protected by a louvered roof with its own independent steel structure.

The lowest level is the family domain, which contains a book-lined hearth and an open kitchen, both of which lie adjacent to the double-height living space. One of the special features of this house is its splendid kitchen, which has been custom-designed to fit the owner's interest in cooking, reflected in the professional appliances and utensils, and a highly efficient extraction system.

All levels of the dwelling are connected by exterior steps in the landscape. These allow direct access to the garden for children, quiet outdoor spaces connected to the parents' study and a private front door for the maid.

The design, which is based on an unusual combination of interior and exterior circulation routes, enables the house to offer occupants an unusual degree of community while also respecting the privacy of the individuals.

PHOTOGRAPHS: DENNIS GILBERT

The external appearance of the building is dominated by a large lattice supported by an independent metal structure.
Access is by a ramp that descends from the roof level into the interior of the dwelling.

Site plan

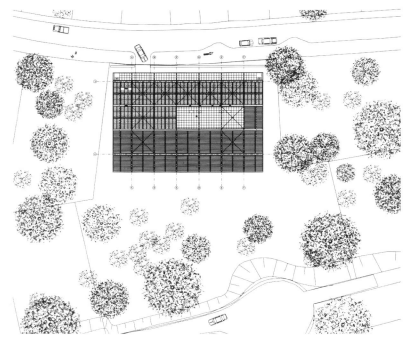

South elevation

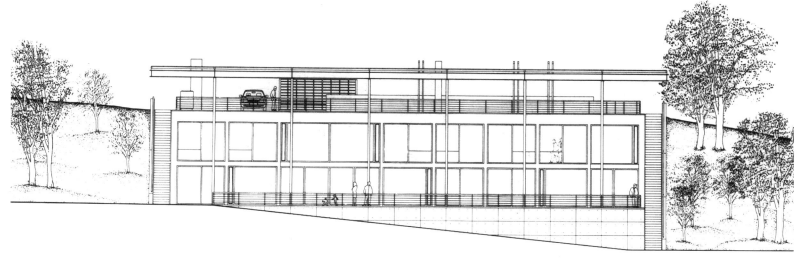

North elevation

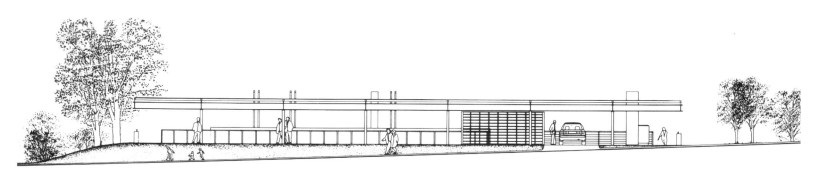

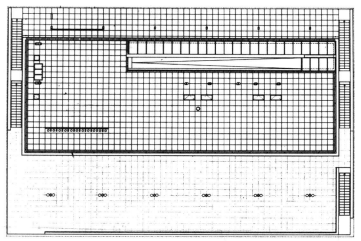

Upper level floor plan

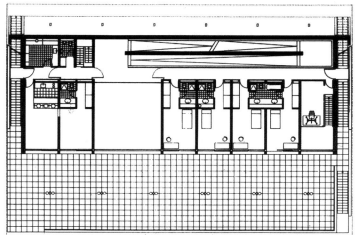

First floor plan

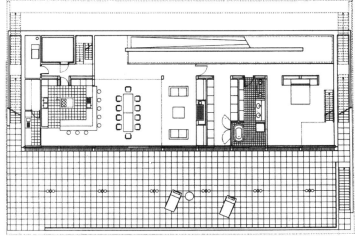

Ground floor plan

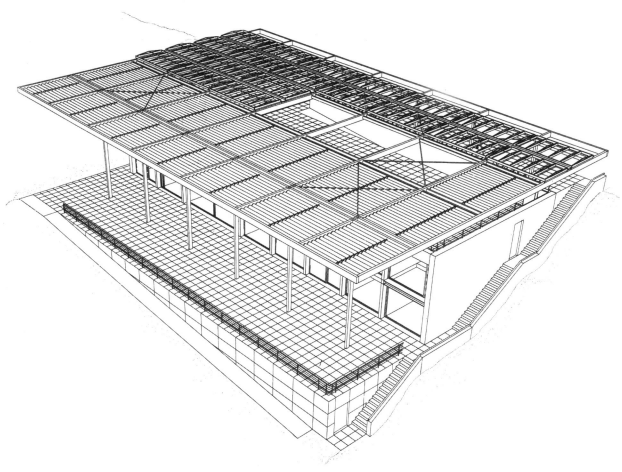

The owner's personal interest in cooking has been translated into an especially meticulous kitchen design. As seen in the photographs, all internal circulation routes are articulated by the access ramp.

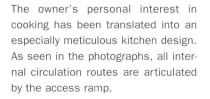

Hiroyuki Arima
House in Dazaifu
Dazaifu, Japan

This house is a device that provides natural views and brings light into the lives of the inhabitants. Here, the value of space focuses on how to give occupants nature rather than functionality and efficiency. That is, it is composed by the combination of some spaces resulting from the consideration of views, light and wind, and life thus follows the order of spaces determined in relation to the exterior. This residence therefore has a standard of value which is apparently different from the ordinary Japanese residence of today, and is much closer to the classical one.

The residence is located not too far from the road to Dazaifu Shrine. The surroundings are silent and do not give the impression that one is close to a tourist spot. The ground here is uneven, and native bamboo groves and broadleaf trees provide pleasing views with the changing seasons. Two boxes are placed on the slope at a difference in level of 10 meters, facing the hills of Dazaifu. Each one is completely independent at its elevation.

The role of the lower box is to cut off the distant views horizontally and to expose the various changes of nature to the interior. Here, the views play an essential part in composing spaces as an element. The interior spaces have no concept of a room. The "box" forms a large room by itself. In it, the small boxes with functional elements, which form the unit arranging the function of life efficiently, have been arranged in an orderly manner. The upper volume also reveals functional elements of the interior.

The upper box opens only vertically, and its role is to separate the interior from the exterior. It consists of two spaces, a light garden with a shallow pool of water, and beyond that is Gallery 2. In this space, the resident can select various light shows by changing operable partitions. If necessary, the interior can be completely separated from the exterior. The visual relationship between man and nature in the upper volume is thus purer than in the lower volume.

The two boxes are connected by a natural path along the inclination of the slope. To live by coming and going between the two volumes means that a part of nature is naturally inserted into the living space.

PHOTOGRAPHS: KOJI OKAMOTO

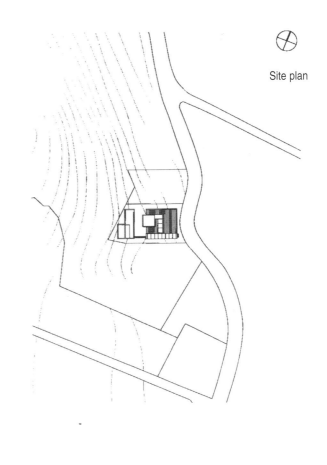

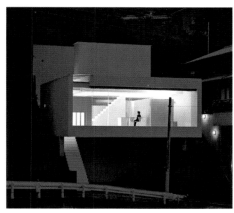

A vertical incision in the main volume
of the dwelling provides natural lighting.

1. Parking
2. Bedroom
3. Kitchen
4. Gallery
5. Light court
6. Music room

Ground floor plan

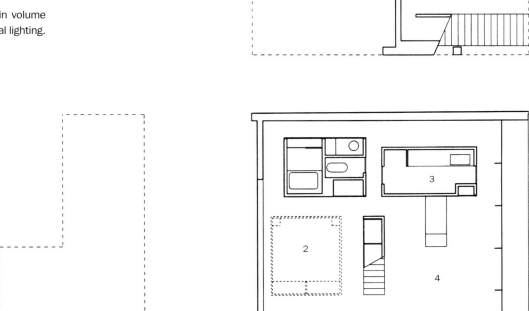

First floor plan

Second floor plan

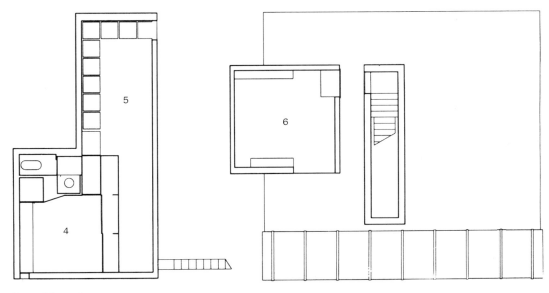

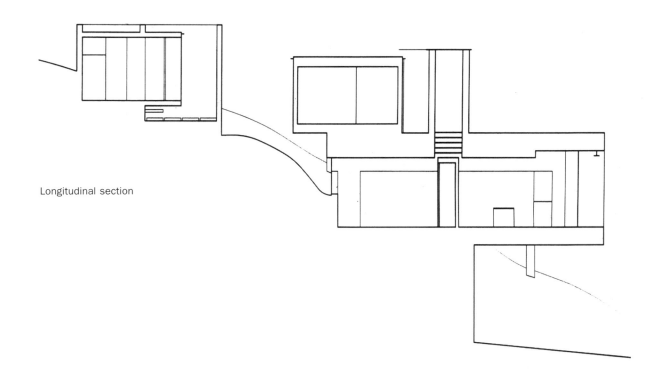

Longitudinal section

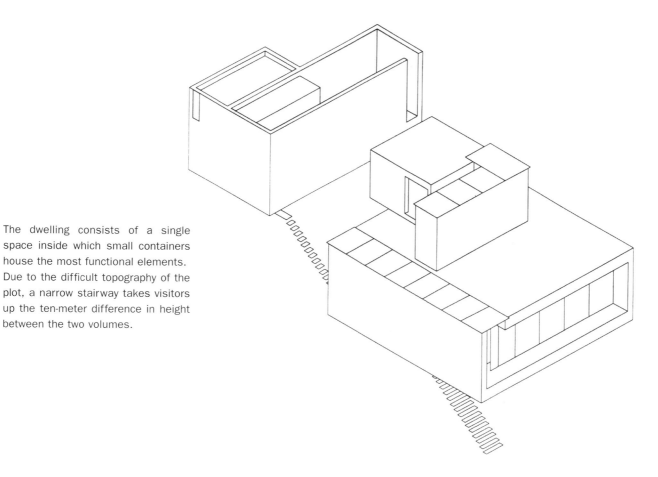

The dwelling consists of a single space inside which small containers house the most functional elements. Due to the difficult topography of the plot, a narrow stairway takes visitors up the ten-meter difference in height between the two volumes.

Architecture Studio
Retirement Residence
Paris, France

This retirement residence for the elderly located in Paris is composed of 83 apartments (with two different floor plans), a supervisor's apartment, communal bathrooms/washrooms, and social areas for the residents.

126 parking spaces are provided within and outside of the complex.

Located in a neighborhood marked by a number of inherent disadvantages, such as small, densely-grouped, non-renovated buildings dating from the early 1900's and earlier, this project for the design of elderly housing contained a directive to show that the area had not been abandoned and that it would be a perfectly safe and desirable area in which to reside.

The high density of buildings and people, narrow streets, and a lack of gardens and open spaces within continuous facades were the conditions that led the architects to construct a low-impact building which would open the center of the parcel of land out toward the city.

The residence is a remarkable achievement in terms of morphology and economy within the city of Paris.

Two scales of use that are both quite important –those of residence and city– are often negatively influenced by a reticence to alter the existing fabric under the pretext that modernity will destroy the city. Fortunately, there are other options to be ventured, as has been shown by the architects in this case.

PHOTOGRAPHS: JEAN MARIE MOTHIERS

General floor plan

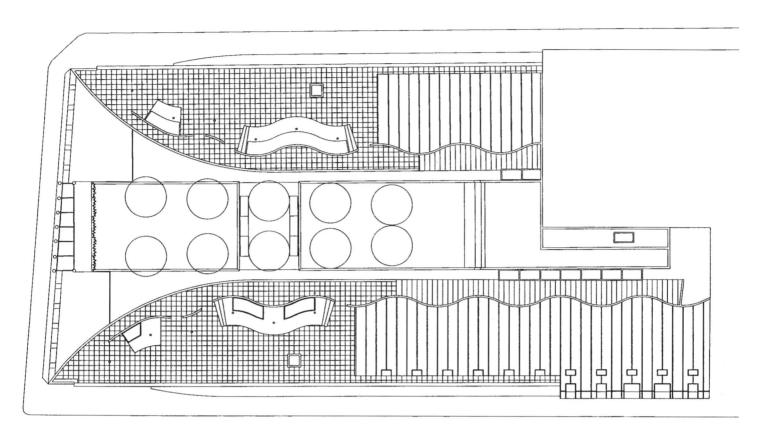

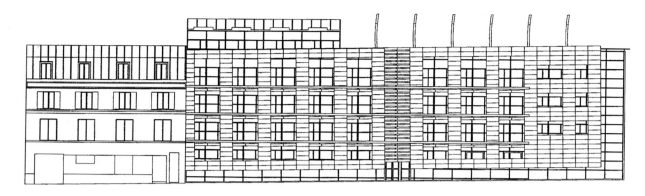

Facade on Desargues street

In order to counteract the high density of the neighborhood and the narrow streets, the project opens onto a patio located in the center of the plot. The volumetric strength and architectural modernity of this residence for the elderly contrast with an aged and barely renovated built environment.

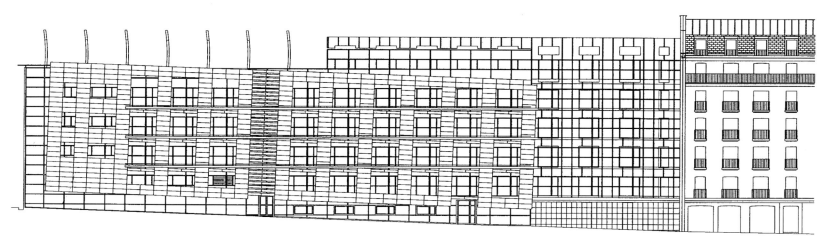

Facade on Morand street

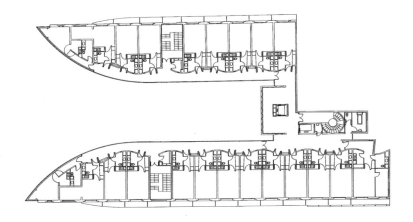

Second floor plan

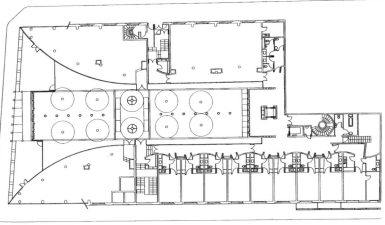

Ground floor plan

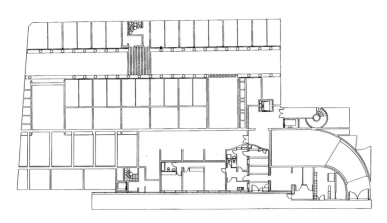

Basement floor plan

Helmut Richter
Wohnanlage Brunner Straße
Vienna, Austria

Brunner Strasse is a main traffic artery leading out of Vienna's southernmost district into the surrounding urban sprawl, with busy industrial locations and reasonably priced residential areas. The growth of private traffic here is far in excess of that of the city itself. The expansion phase, which started in Vienna at the beginning of the 1990s, has long come to an end. The surroundings of this building suggest a development that has encountered difficulties. Differences in the age of the built substance, in the use of sites and the density of development dominate the situation. On the one hand, Atzgersdorf still offers, here and there, a lively residential situation; on the other, the industrial area, Liesing, which can be reached in a few minutes on foot and is therefore part of the residents' consciousness, reveals itself as an inadequate technocratic occupation of the territory.

For this exposed and, therefore, inexpensive site, the client, a communal body, sought by means of direct commissioning a housing design which naturally had to meet certain requirements in order to obtain the state housing subsidy. The architect later expressed his doubts about the logic of placing a building on this site, but he responded to the ambivalent circumstances with an extreme formulation of the deck access type. He satisfied the residents' need for protection with a circulation system placed as a buffer between the apartments and the street, while also thematically treating their exposure in urban space. The periphery as a non-place is radicalised, its contradictions are made visible and, as a result, it becomes inhabitable. It is the conflict, conducted in an open and unorthodox manner, between a sense of calm and movement, which permits the development of an identifiable place in the diffuse mix on the city's outskirts. Richter's basic principles of high quality housing and living, characterized by "clarity and simplicity of organization" that he earlier demonstrated in the project for the Gräf & Stift grounds become concrete in the Brunner Strasse design. Consciously balanced spatial qualities and reference aim at "leaving it up to the individual to choose communication or isolation" for, in the architect's opinion, these are "the most important criteria with regard to living and human existence". Housing and urban development are closely linked to each other. Housing is the end zone of a hierarchical sequence of spaces, it connects the most public element, the city, and the most private, the space to withdraw to in the dwelling. It can expand the social dimensions of being or restrict them. According to the architect, housing is an allegory of the position of the individual in the family and society as expressed in architecture.

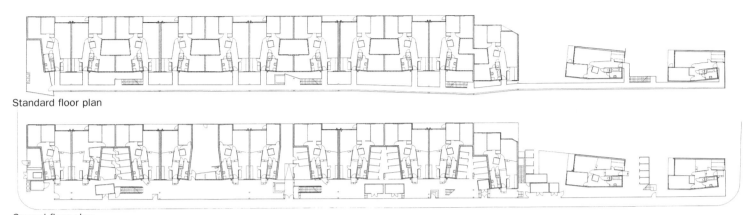

Standard floor plan

Ground floor plan

The architect sought to lessen the impact of the high density caused by heavy traffic flow and a narrow foot-path in front of the housing block. A circulation route serves as a buffer between the dwellings and the street noise.

Floor to ceiling wall openings –aluminum-framed windows and sliding doors– seem to dissolve the boundaries between interior and exterior.

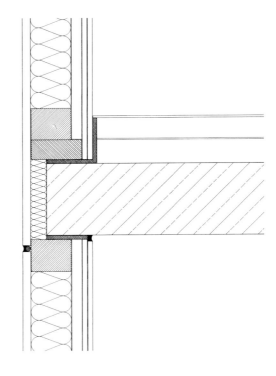

Construction detail

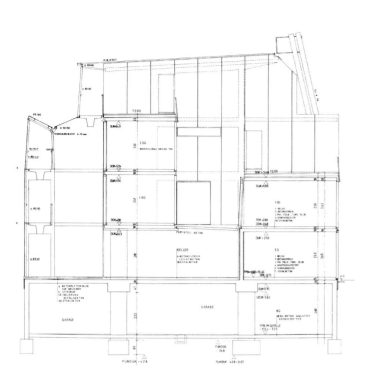

Cross section

FOBA / Katsu Umebayashi
Aura House
Tokyo, Japan

In the amorphous complexity of central Tokyo, urban structure occurs at scales imperceptible to the pedestrian observer. Forms are either incoherent or irrelevant; the urban experience is a succession of interior spaces.

Here, a house requires few facilities. To eat, you go to a restaurant; to bathe, you go to the *sento* (public baths); to exercise, you go to the gym; for entertainment, you go to the cinema. The ultimate Tokyo house is somehow like an art gallery: an empty, inward-looking space, perhaps with unusual lighting.

The Aura house is located in a typical Japanese "eel's nest" site: an alley measuring 3.5m width by 21.5m length. The challenge was to bring light and air into the center of the house. Rather than using the traditional *tsubo-niwa* (courtyard garden), the architects opted instead for optimizing both the available light and the potential floor area.

Concrete walls were run down either side of the site and a translucent membrane was stretched between them. In order to sustain tension in the roof fabric, a complex curve was created by making the two walls identical in contour, only reversed. Cylindrical concrete beams brace the two walls. The opposing ridge lines cause the orientation of the beams to twist along the length of the building which is, despite appearances, a rational structural solution. The fabric skin filters sunlight by day, and glows by night: the building pulses, "breathing" light with the 24-hour rhythm of the city.

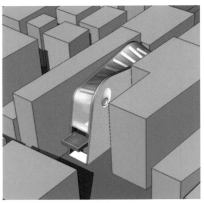

PHOTOGRAPHS: TOHRU WAKI (SHOKOKUSHA PUB. CO., LTD.)

The plot is wedged into an alley, which is 3.5m wide by 21.5m long. Rather than using the traditional *tsubo-niwa* (courtyard garden), the architects opted instead for optimizing both the available light and the potential floor area.

Site plan

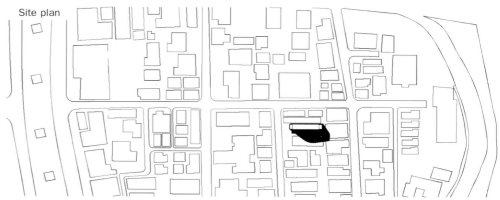

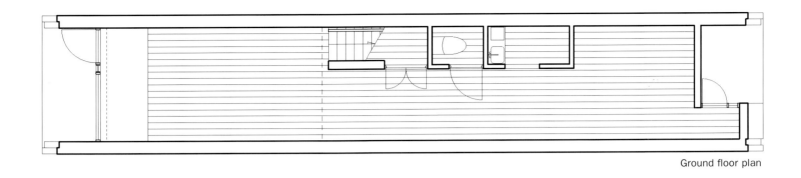

Ground floor plan

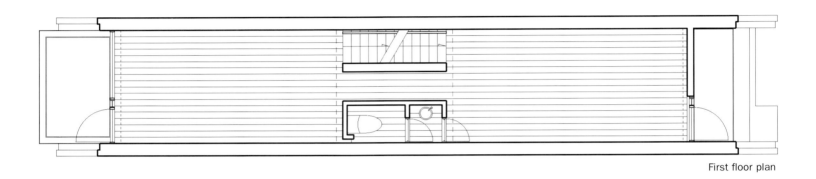

First floor plan

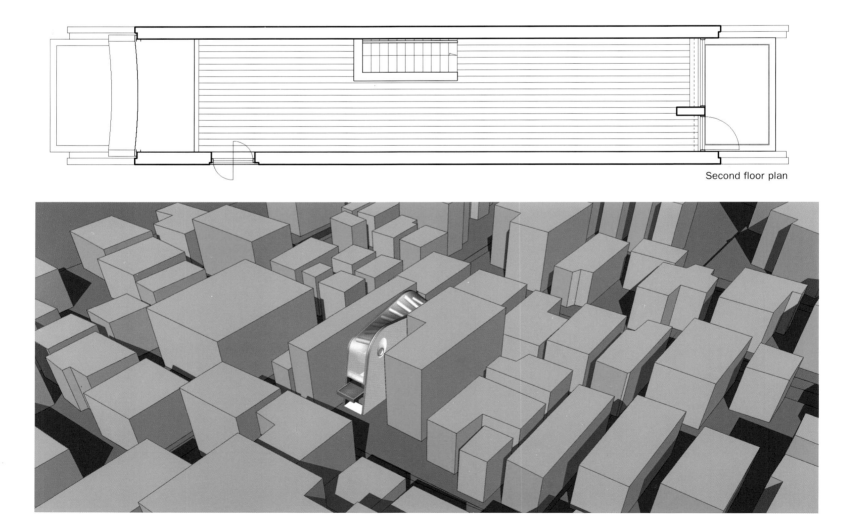

Second floor plan

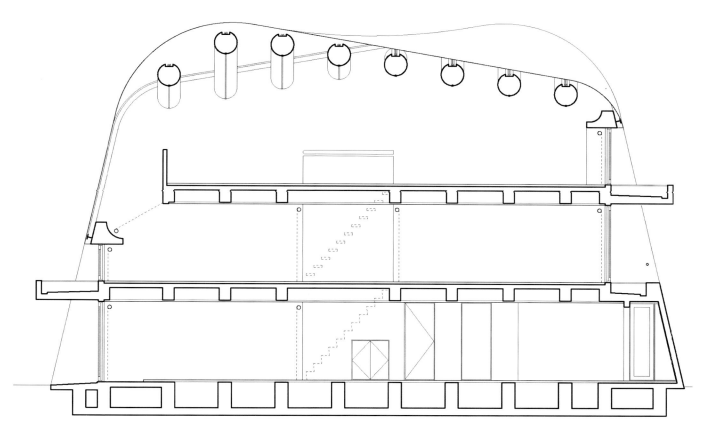

Longitudinal section

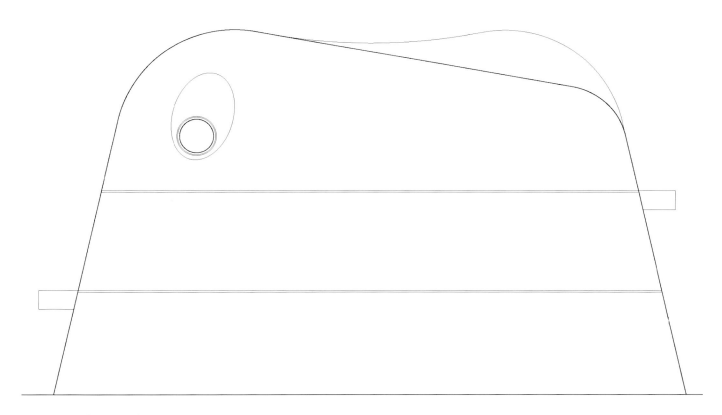

Side elevation

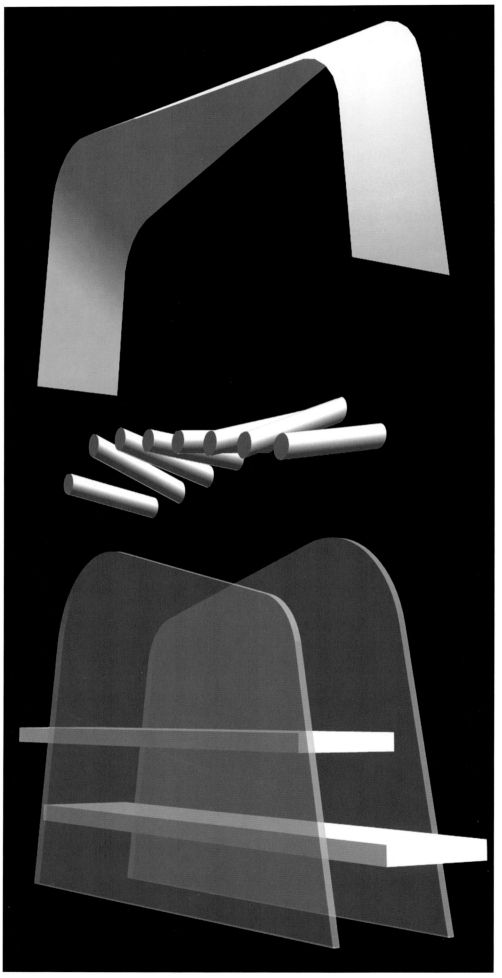

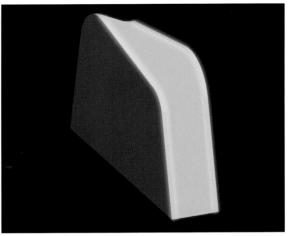

Concrete walls were run down either side of the site and a translucent membrane was stretched between them. In order to sustain tension in the roof fabric, a curve was created by making the two walls identical but reversed. Cylindrical concrete beams brace the two walls.

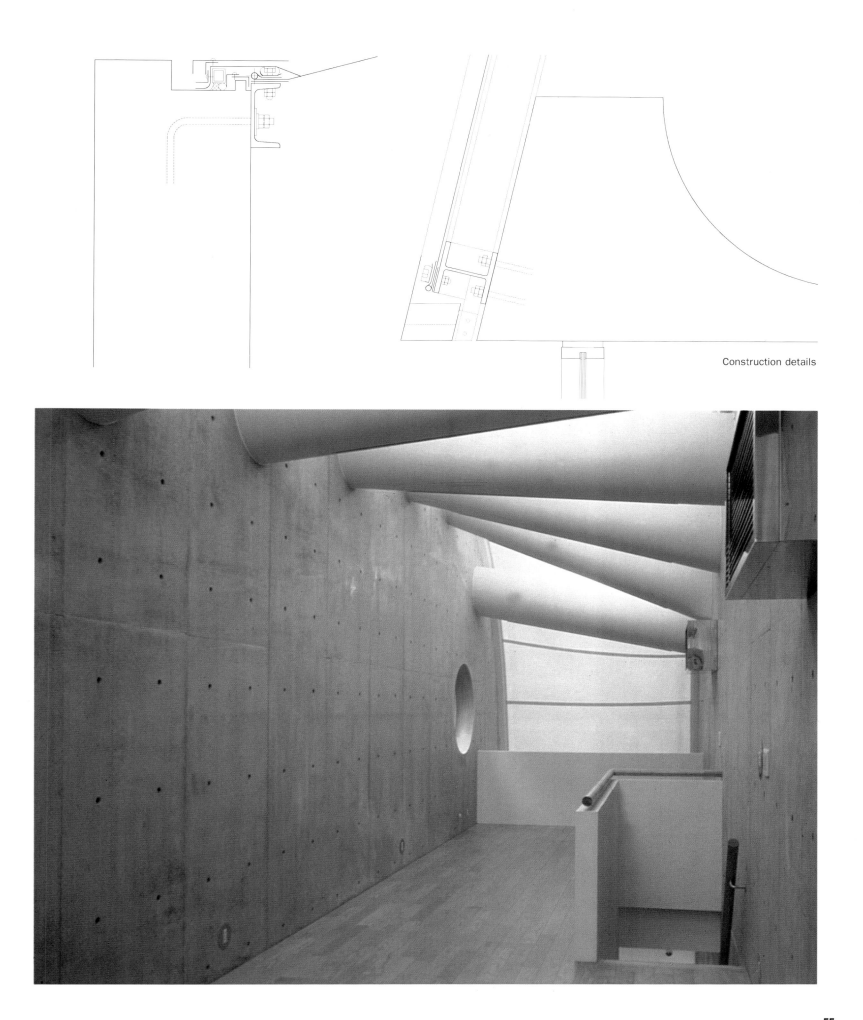

Construction details

Jean-Paul Bonnemaison
Maison en Lubéron
Lubéron, France

The building is strategically located beside a church in a small village in Haute Provence, with good views of the street and the adjoining fields. The dwelling was built on the ruins of an old oil mill with the intention of preserving the memory of what was formerly one of the main sources of wealth in the area. It fits perfectly into the building codes of this village, conserving several external walls and following a program based on the urban volumetrics that amplify the perspectives of the main street, thus respecting the style of the neighboring buildings and the dominance of the church.

The small, sharply sloping plot is fully occupied by terraces and gardens crossed by a path that leads to an existing swimming pool. The facades are clearly differentiated, and the public facade faces the town with five stone steps that emphasize the main entrance. The circular windows in the wall provide privacy and give the residents splendid views of the church steeple and castle. This facade has a stone structure and has been architecturally intensified by means of jalousie windows that offer views of the town whilst protecting the interior from excessive sunlight. The other facade, facing the fields, is private and totally glazed. Its design faithfully represents the changes of a society: new materials and construction systems combined with respect for nature.

The project is broken down horizontally into two groups, one containing services and the guest area, and the other containing the main rooms of the house. Vertically, this main group consists of four levels, the last one with a bedroom, bathroom and terrace. The living room occupies three levels, with terraces that ensure spatial continuity with the sloping garden. A metal staircase connects the different levels. The incorporation of this element on the glazed facade combines with the environment and allows the inhabitants to enjoy a different room, sitting in it as if it were a theater.

The interior design is governed by the elegant and simple requirements of the clients, who are fascinated by Cistercian art, and includes hints of minimalism. The interior walls were painted white to capture the natural light of Provence and to highlight the collection of sketches that decorate the house. The light-colored stone, the bluish grey of the structure and the beige of the cement areas fit into the general coloring of the town whilst giving the house its own unique character.

PHOTOGRAPHS: LEONAR DE SELVA

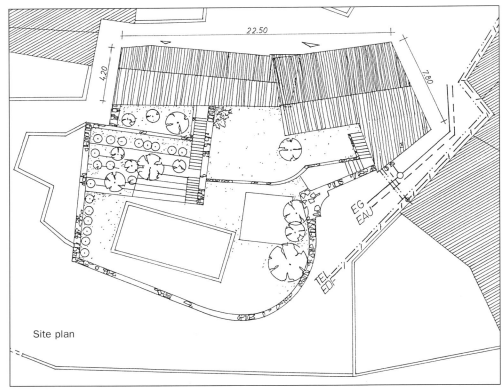

Site plan

The prime location of this dwelling and the absence of other buildings in front of the glazed facade allow the light to enter unhindered and give the landscape a dominant role.

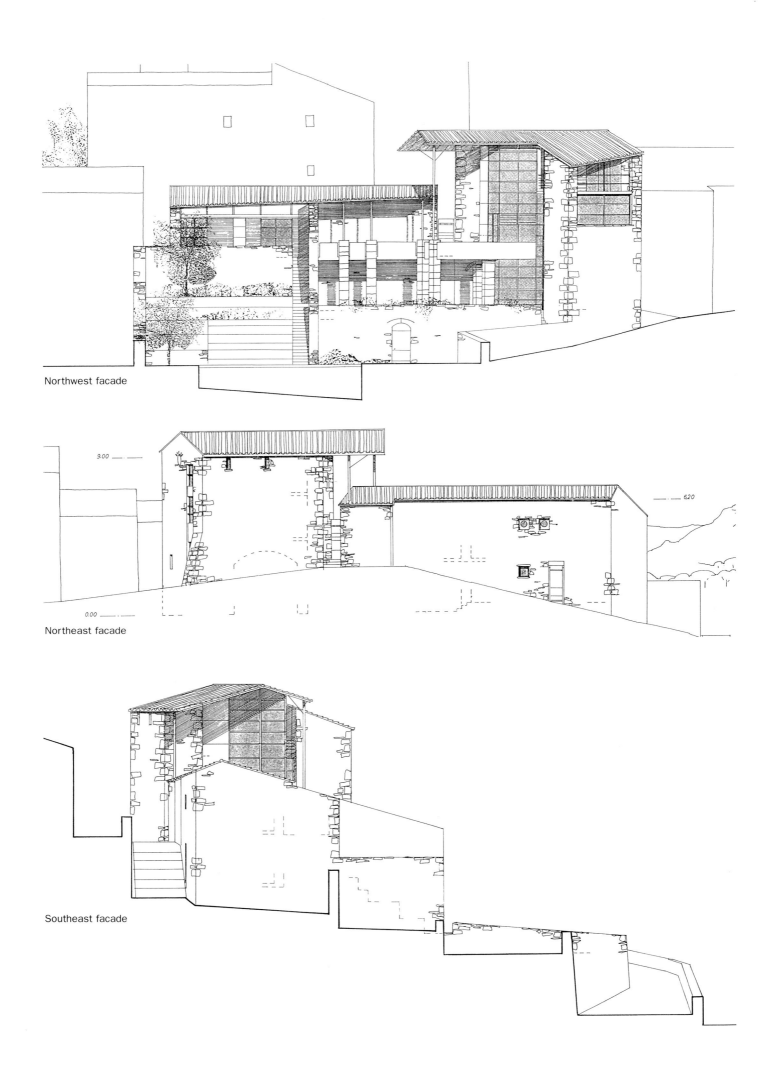

Northwest facade

9.00

0.00

Northeast facade

6.20

Southeast facade

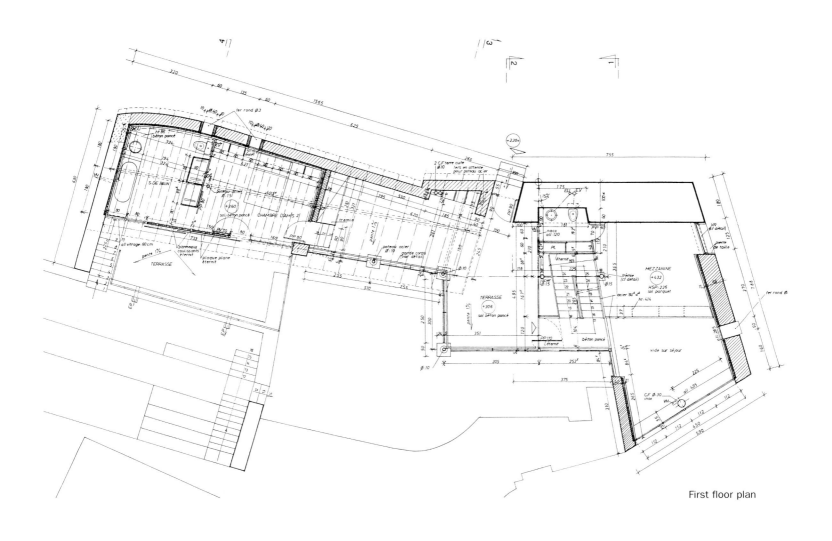

First floor plan

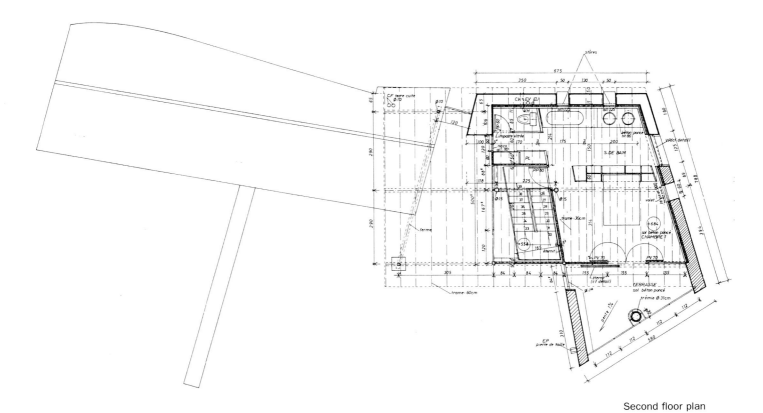

Second floor plan

The broken form of the staircase provides a continuous solution to the great difference in level between the floors of the dwelling. Its situation in front of the window converts it into a kind of a tier from which one can contemplate the landscape and the interior space.

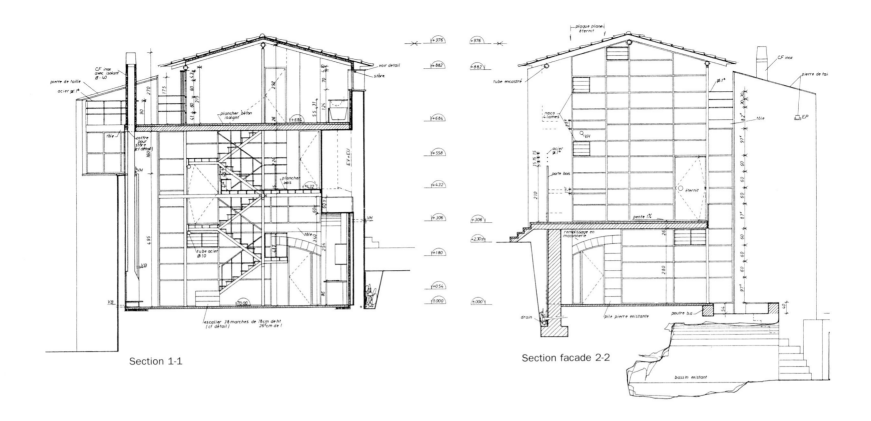

Section 1-1

Section facade 2-2

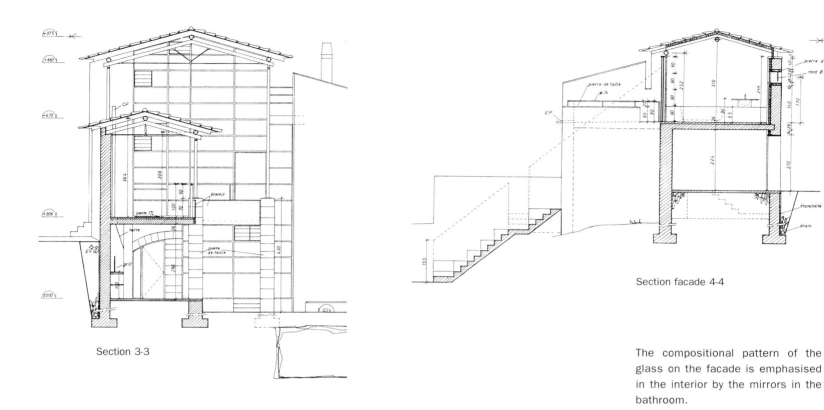

Section 3-3

Section facade 4-4

The compositional pattern of the glass on the facade is emphasised in the interior by the mirrors in the bathroom.

Helin & Siitonen
Experimental House
Boras, Sweden

PHOTOGRAPHS: TITA LUMIO

Living at the dawn of a new century calls for a new approach to planning new housing solutions, and new types of houses. This experimental house is formed by two wedges with an atrium between them; i.e. an extended stairwell forming a central common area.

All apartments are entered through this area on the ground level, through the staircase and corridors, or using the private stairs directly to the second floor apartments. The connections with the existing human landscape and verdant nature formed the basis of the design of this house. The same principle has been followed in the whole Hestra area, in order to minimize the changes in the landscape.

The house includes 24 one-level apartments of 63m² (3 rooms and a kitchen), and ten two-level apartments on the top floor, two of them of 83m² (8 rooms and a kitchen) and eight of them of 97m² (4 rooms and a kitchen). These two-level apartments have a sauna and terrace on the roof. The foyer and the kitchen are located along the atrium, but the bedrooms and the living room are along the more private and quiet outer side of the wedge. The apartments are flexible and highly functional in a variety of living conditions and differing lifestyles.

The framework of the building is reinforced concrete; the facades and the floor slabs are of pre-fabricated concrete. To emphasize the connection with nature, this building has a turf roof. All vertical facilities, air conditioning, plumbing and electrical installations, are assembled on the facades around the atrium, making them accessible for service and changes.

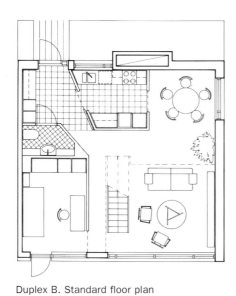

Duplex B. Standard floor plan

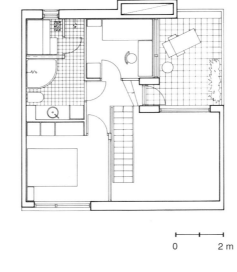

0   2 m

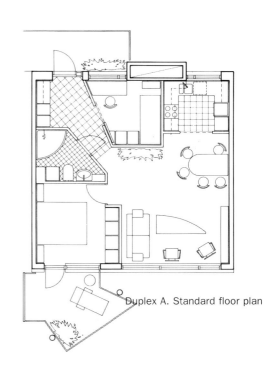

Duplex A. Standard floor plan

Site plan

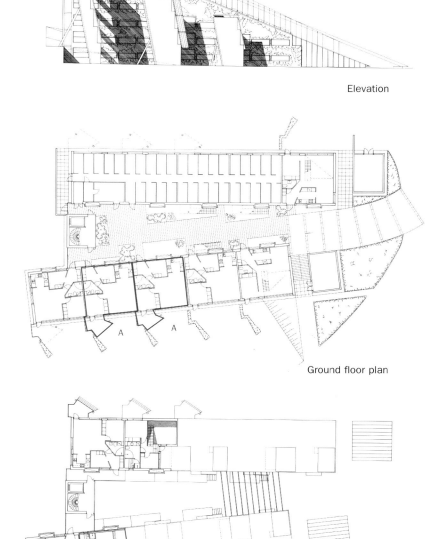

Elevation

Ground floor plan

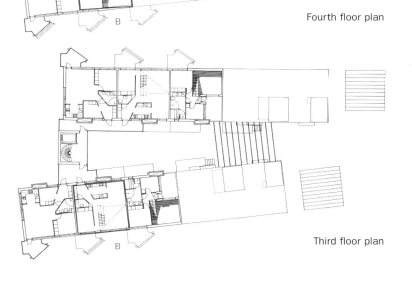

Fourth floor plan

Third floor plan

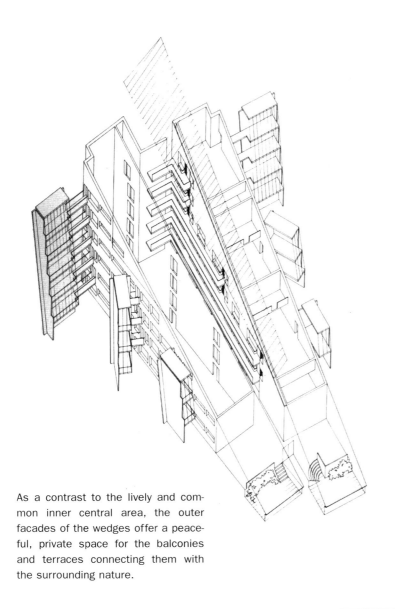

As a contrast to the lively and common inner central area, the outer facades of the wedges offer a peaceful, private space for the balconies and terraces connecting them with the surrounding nature.

Shinichi Ogawa & Associates
Glass House
Hiroshima, Japan

The building is located in the western part of the Japanese city of Hiroshima, known as Nishi Ward. This area lies on the estuary of the Hachiman River where it discharges into the Seto Inland Sea.

This is a very pure and geometrical volume, a minimal and open glass box that contains at the same time the house and the studio of the architect Shinichi Ogawa.

The project is based on a three-meter, three-dimensional grid and takes the simple form of a 6x15x12 m box. The volume is divided into four parts along its Z-axis, with the two uppermost blocks (6x15x12 m) forming the third floor, where the architectural office is located, and the two lower blocks constituting the first and second floor living spaces.

The different living areas are divided by furniture and partitions, and the spaces have a neutral quality, allowing flexibility with respect to changing functional requirements.

The building is wrapped in transparent glass on all four facades, which strongly contributes to making the interior a very sunny and clean space during the daytime. Nevertheless, all the spaces can be enclosed, if desired, using movable insulating screens that change the perception of the building from the outside as well.

West elevation

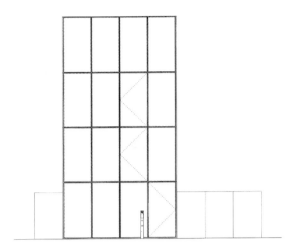

South elevation

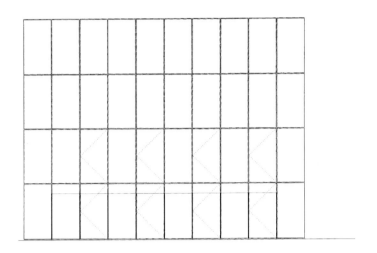

Cross-section

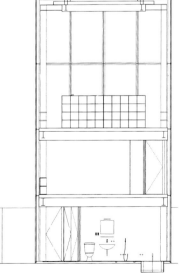

The house, based on a three-dimensional scheme, takes on the form of a glass box of 6x15x12 m. Vertically, it is divided into four parts. Located on the upper floor, the office occupies the two uppermost volumes while the two lower parts encompass the two floors of dwellings.

East elevation

North elevation

Second floor plan

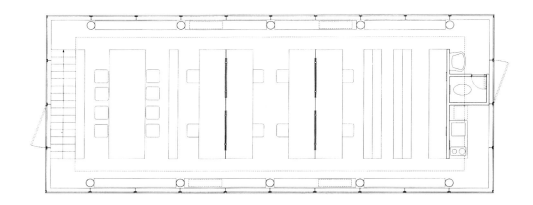

First floor plan

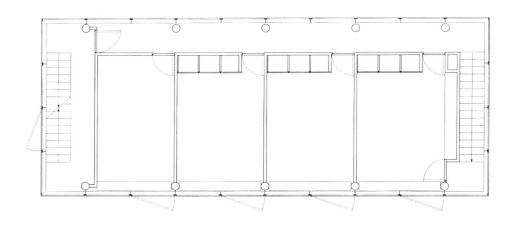

Ground floor plan

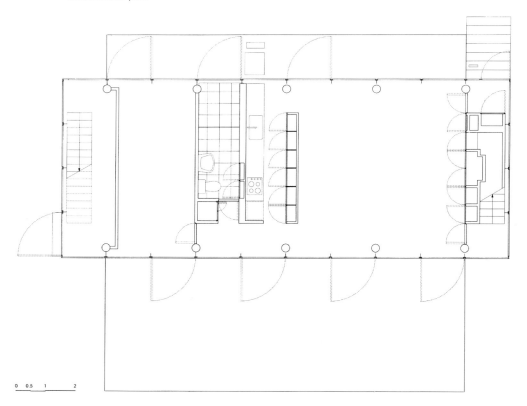

0   0.5   1   2

The building is wrapped in transparent glass on all four facades, which strongly contributes to making the interior a very sunny and clean space during the daytime.

The level of privacy and solar protection can be increased on the four transparent glass facades by the use of curtains.

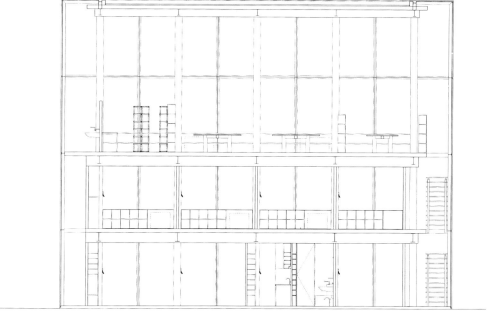

0 05 1   2

Benson + Forsyth
Marico Factory and Residence
London, UK

Located in Islington on the north bank of the Grand Union Canal, the site consisted of the shell of a derelict factory and two cottages. The single-story walls of the canal towpath and the gardens to the north, together with the two-story cottage walls which face the park and the existing houses, have been retained. Within the house a metal valley-roof supported on perforated metal troughs and a steel frame is carried centrally on two pairs of steel columns. Externally the roof is reminiscent of a traditional Islington valley-roof, while internally it reads as a free-standing umbrella dissociated from the perimeter walls and independent of the galleries and volumes below.

The ground floor is occupied by the principal living spaces, which relate to the studio across the courtyard, or internally through the single-story dining/conference room, which may be used in conjunction with both the studio and the living floor. The first-floor gallery contains a second living space: a dressing room and bedroom which overlook the park and the canal and extend onto the roof terrace over the single-story link into the office gallery within the studio.

The upper floor is composed of two cubes: the bathroom within a 2.1 meter cube made of opal white glass, and the main bedroom, which is located in a roof-lit enclosure suspended over the lower sitting area.

The design of the workshop section was governed by the need to maintain the two-story enclosure of the adjacent buildings on the canal side and to keep the level of the roof below the single-story wall of the gardens on the north. The roof and all of the wall planes are dissociated by glazing which washes the planes with indirect light.

PHOTOGRAPHS: HÉLÈNE BINET

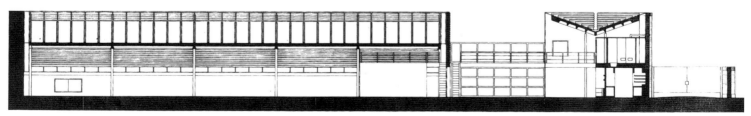

Section BB

0   2m

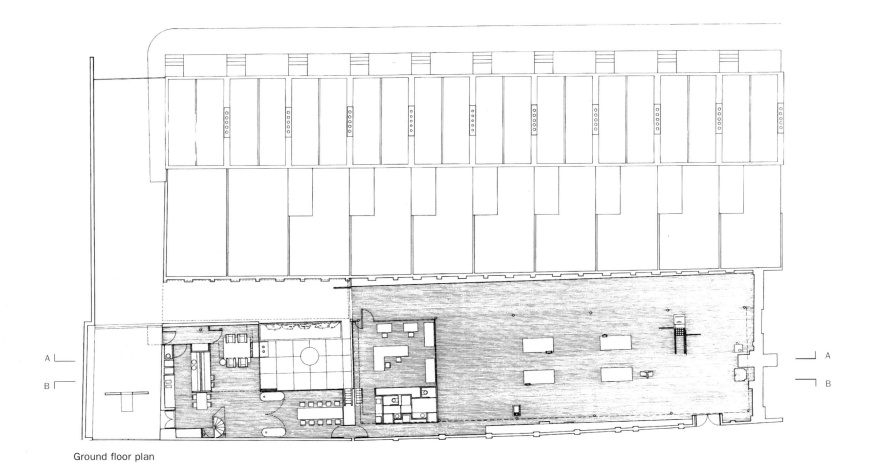

Ground floor plan

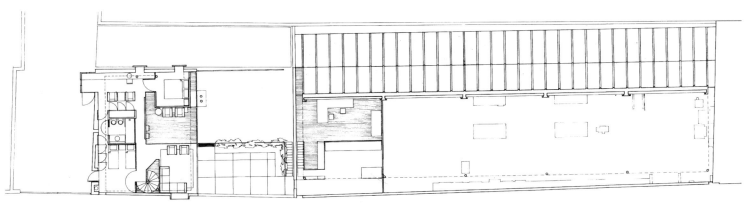

First floor plan

0   2m

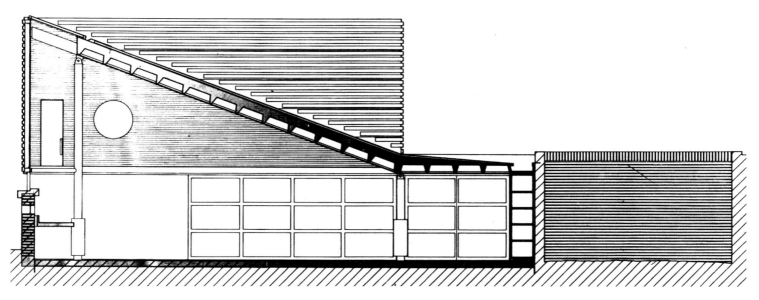

Cross section

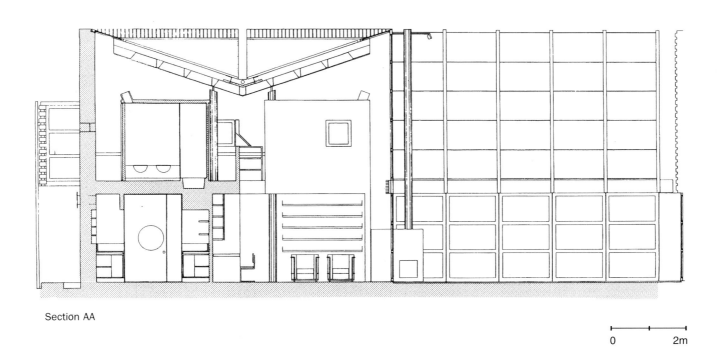

Section AA

0   2m

A metal valley-roof supported on perforated metal troughs and a steel frame is carried on two pairs of steel columns. This structure is dissociated from the perimeter walls and independent of the galleries and volumes below.

Axonometric view

Georges Maurios Architecte D.U.H.
Montenegro House
Paris, France

The architect, originally reticent to take on this project because of spatial and budgetary restrictions, was eventually seduced by the unique challenge that it offered. The 7x12-meter plot of land was hemmed in tightly between two party walls and, at the back, there was a 4.5-meter-high, south-facing separating wall which had to be retained. Furthermore, the derelict framework of an abandoned construction was still on the site.

In spite of the setbacks, a spacious four-story home was achieved. A maximum of volume and floor area was capitalized on by the use of very economical and technically improved materials such as steel, wood and sandwich panels. Many of the elements were prefabricated off-site, transported in and simply pieced together. The structure was fairly lightweight and therefore did not require a complex and expensive foundation.

The ground plan of the house consists of two distinct parts: on one side a 2-meter-wide strip accommodates the staircase, kitchen, laundry, and all of the bathrooms and toilets, while the other side (5 meters wide) consists of living areas, a lounge, bedrooms and a studio.

The living room, part of which is double height, is connected to the kitchen and the stairwell so that it forms the dwelling's spatial center and occupies the entire first floor. It is extended outside onto the wooden terrace overlooking one end of a narrow garden.

The entire structure is based on steel columns and beams. The skeleton is visible on the inside, where it complements the overall industrial feel of the house. The floors have been made from 140mm-thick galvanized steel panels, which are also in tune with the aesthetic quality of the whole building as well as enhancing the acoustic quality of the individual spaces. The walls and roof are clad in insulated steel panels.

PHOTOGRAPHS: GASTON & JEAN-MARIE MONTHIERS

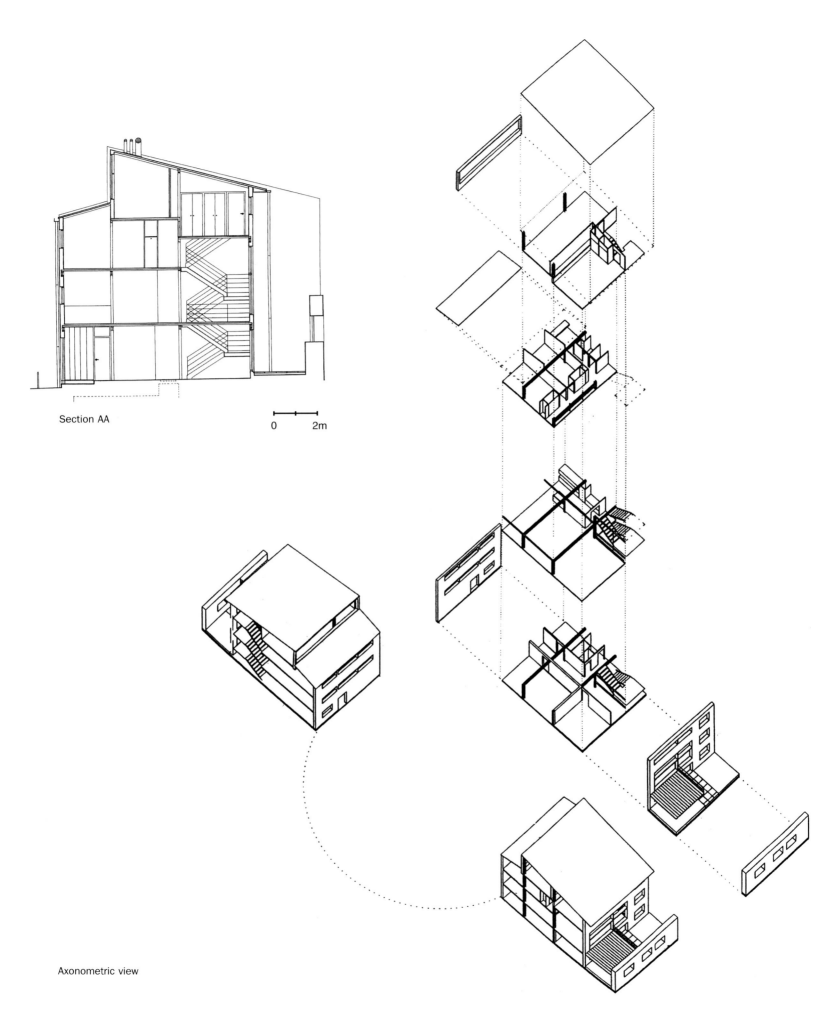

Section AA

0   2m

Axonometric view

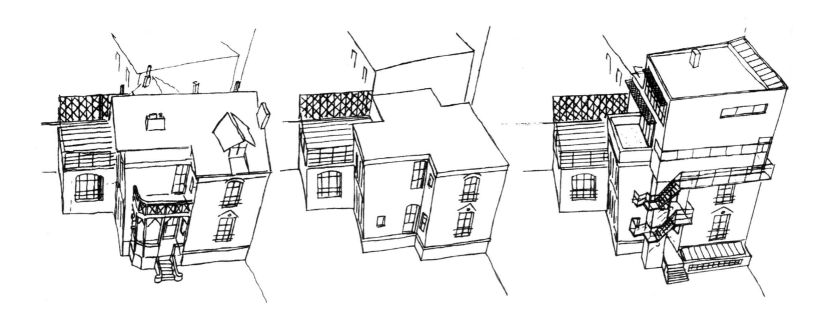

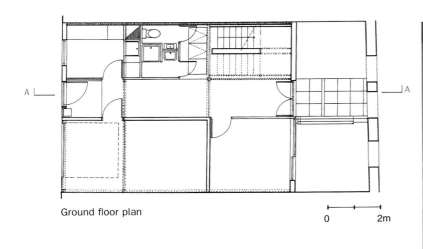

Ground floor plan

0   2m

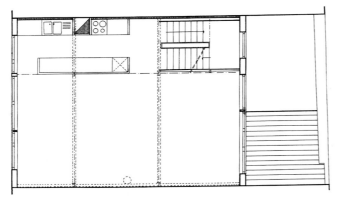

First floor plan

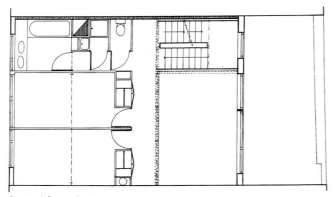

Second floor plan

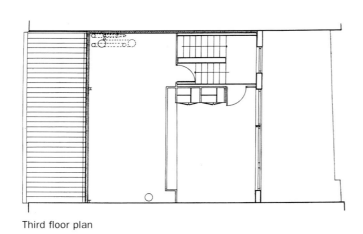

Third floor plan

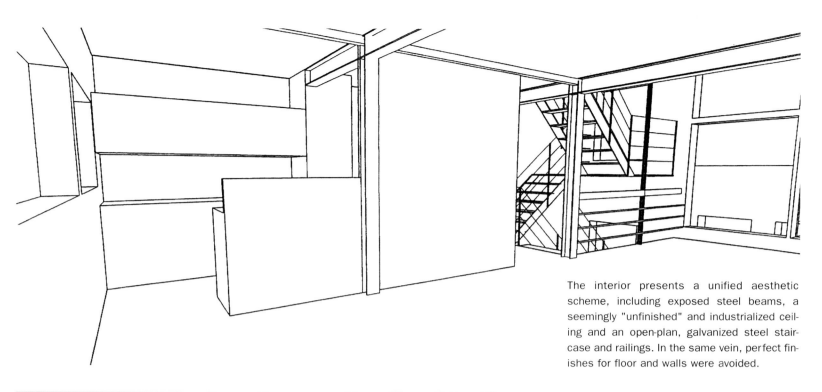

The interior presents a unified aesthetic scheme, including exposed steel beams, a seemingly "unfinished" and industrialized ceiling and an open-plan, galvanized steel staircase and railings. In the same vein, perfect finishes for floor and walls were avoided.

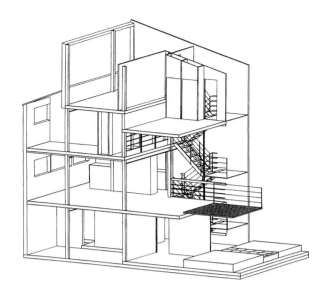

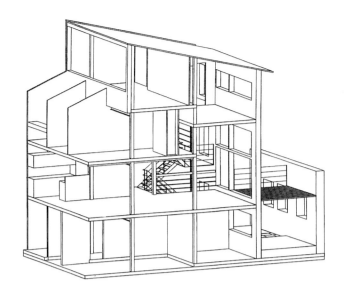

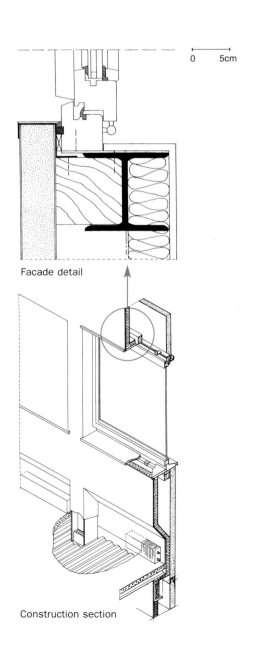

Facade detail

Construction section

Felix Claus & Kees Kaan

Housing Haarlemmerbuurt

Amsterdam, The Netherlands

Where the former harbors of Amsterdam meet the "Canal belt" we find the "Haarlemmerbuurt", a lively neighborhood set between the water of the Y-river and the bourgeois atmosphere of the canals.

The architects carried out several small projects in this area. The existing monuments were restored and combined in one project with a new infill. In medical terminology one would call the operation one of microsurgery.

In the case of Binnen Wieringerstraat, the existing structure, which was in an extremely degraded condition, was only 3.5 meters wide and 8 meters deep and set on a rectilinear site made trapezoidal by the street. Thus, the floor plan and inner wall are orthogonal, while the elevation lies askew. In fact, this is typical of Amsterdam, where there are many discrepancies between the street facades and projecting mechanisms.

The architects decided to use the adjacent small plot to build a new structure, leaving the old structure to house contemporary, loft-type living spaces. The new structure contains all the more private and technical functions: vertical circulation, storage, and a single bath and bedroom per floor. The monument contains three bedrooms.

The architects call this an "infusion" or "drip". In this manner they could preserve the old structure with its essential monumental detailing without having to alter it for installations, shafts or staircases.

Instead of ending up with the monument as an inhabitable museum, it is a free space of 7x3 meters, a luxury in social housing. All that is necessary to meet contemporary standards is placed inside the drip.

The facade of the drip is carefully designed to avoid typical "social housing" associations. Lying almost flush with the street elevation is a new screen of three large sheets of glass. It is shocking and seductive, with fluorescent tubes (concealed behind the metal section) illuminating the vivid yellow of the interior wall. The surface of each glazing panel is divided into translucent and transparent areas so that the public cannot quite read the circular stairs behind. Finally the glass folds inwards on top so that this sheer and rather cinematic foyer is also bathed in top lighting.

The surface of each glazing panel is divided into translucent and transparent areas so that the public cannot quite read the circular stairs behind.

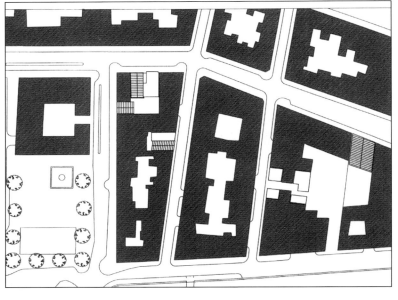

Site plan

Main elevation

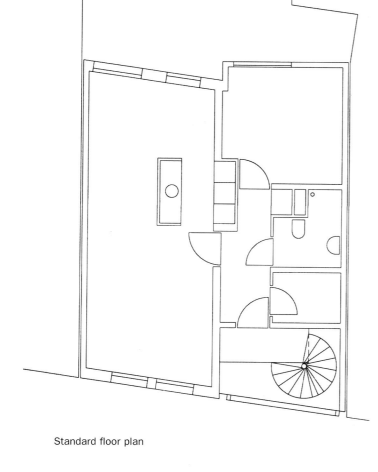

Standard floor plan

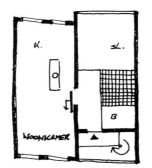

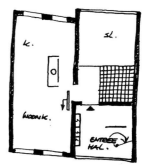

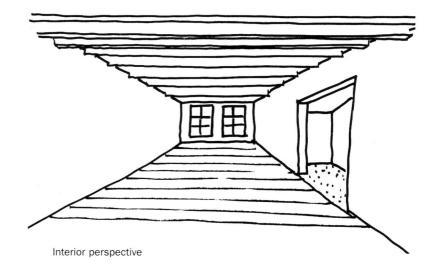

Interior perspective

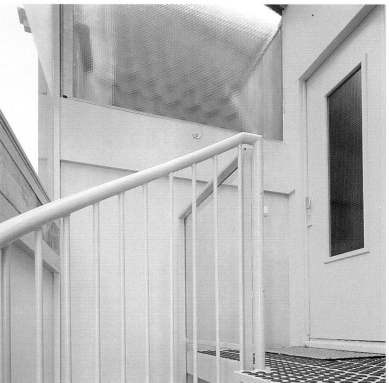

Koh Kitayama + architecture WORKSHOP
Plane + House
Tokyo, Japan

This house, with an attached studio and a total floor area of 177m², occupies almost the entirety of its small plot, located in a densely populated area of Tokyo. The client is an industrial designer who required that the building include facilities for both a home and office.

Because of local zoning restrictions the construction area is an exact square, which at least offers the possibility of creating wide-open, diaphanous spaces. The building is an equal span rigid-frame structure with supporting columns on the inside, freeing up space in the hallways.

The space formed between the outer and inner walls is used for staircases, and also serves as a ventilation duct. Top-lit glass has been installed in the ceiling in this space, guiding natural light downwards.

This structure displays the planar format of homes often seen in Asia, with hallways running around the outside of the living areas. Such spaces are easily adaptable to changes in daily living.

However, in other aspects, the architects have consciously tried to distance the design of this biulding from typical Japanese architecture. They feel that in the past several years, particularly in Japan, there has been a trend towards an almost unnatural sterility and homogeneity, reminiscent of the brightly-lit convenience store equipped with air conditioning and heating. Homes in which spatial composition and environment-friendly technology support one another are not —but perhaps shoud be— the norm. As a response, they have designed a home in which the occupants must recognize when it is time for a "change of clothes", opening and closing household fixtures according to the given climate and season.

PHOTOGRAPHS: NOBUAKI NAKAGAWA

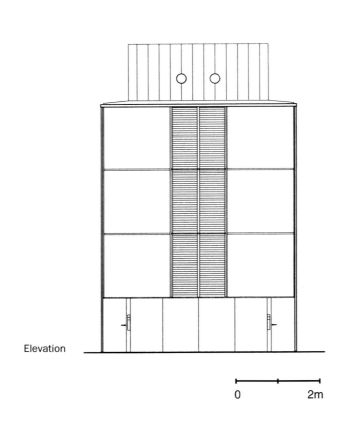

Elevation

0   2m

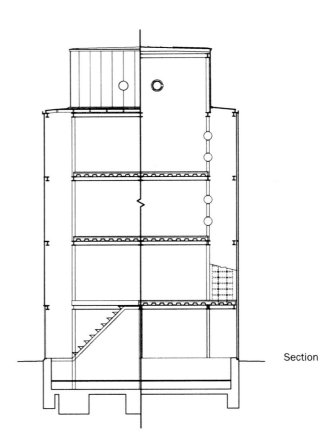

Section

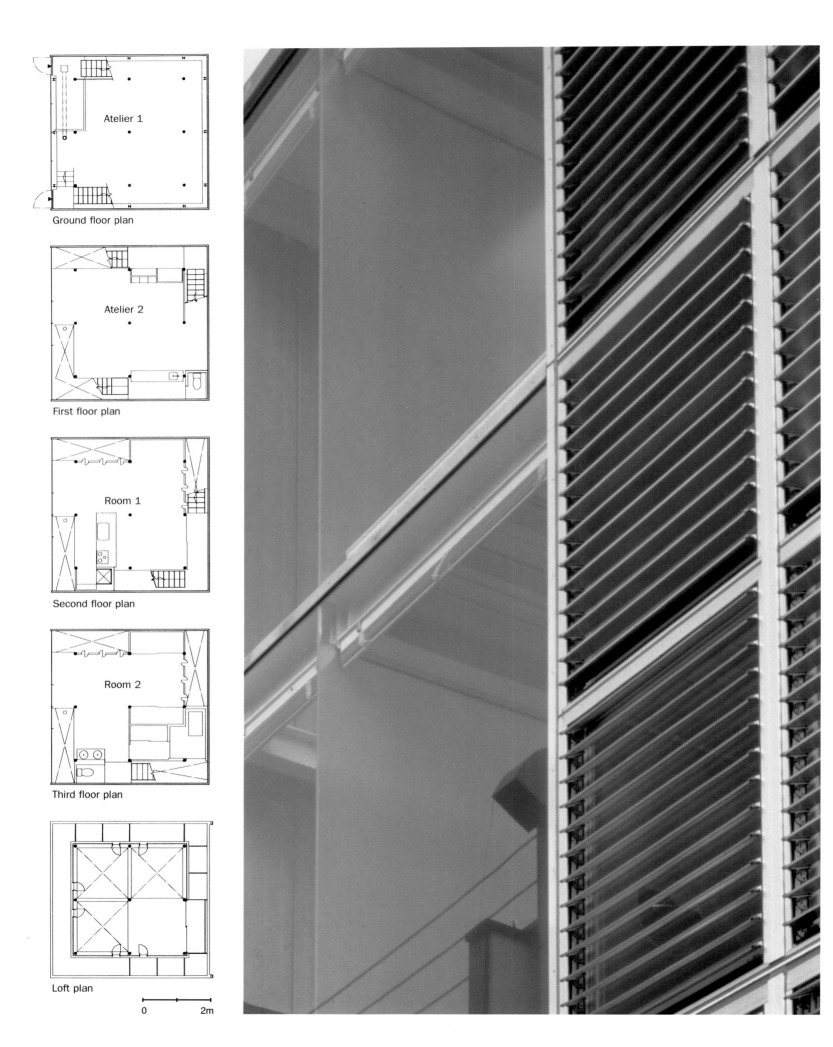

Atelier 1

Ground floor plan

Atelier 2

First floor plan

Room 1

Second floor plan

Room 2

Third floor plan

Loft plan

0   2m

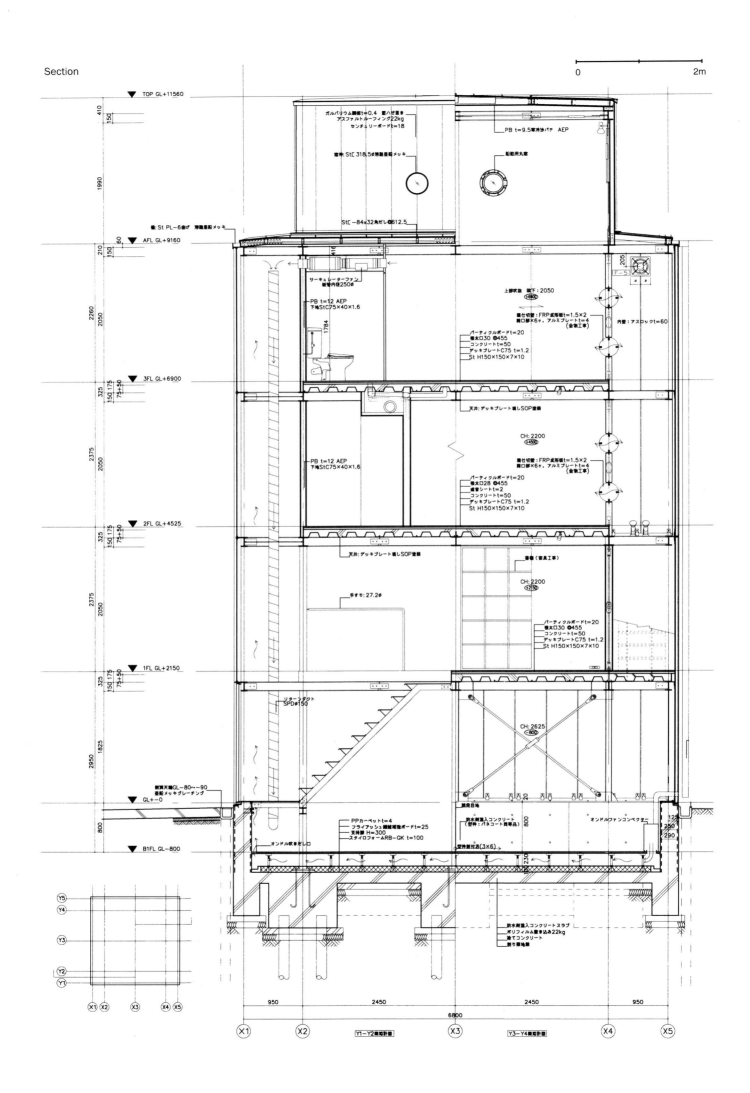

Section

Due to zoning laws, the construction space is an exact square, a limitation which nonetheless gave rise to the creation of wide-open spaces. Hallways and stairways have been placed on the periphery of the living areas.

Glenn Murcutt
Studio house for artists
Sydney, Australia

The building, a long metal volume with a light appearance and large windows that open onto the landscape, is set on a plot that is staggered in the form of sandstone terraces, inside a natural park near the Australian capital. One of the fundamental requirements of the project was to establish a respectful dialogue between the new building and the natural environment. For this reason, it was decided to place the house on fourteen slender columns that are anchored into the rock and reduce direct contact of the volume with the ground.

The facades overhang the sequence of columns, emphasizing the impression of a light structure that communicates with the ground by means of a walkway that meets the volume diagonally on one of its long facades.

Two porches, located on the long sides of the volume, extend the surface of the base platform of the construction and help to establish a powerful dialogue with the natural environment. Another of the most important points in the project is the meticulous study of fire protection measures.

The wood that covers the base of the volume was coated with a layer of fire-retarding paint and a series of sprinklers on the roof ensure protection in the event of fire.

The owners of the dwelling, a couple of painters, asked the architect to bear in mind their activity and consider a series of naked surfaces on which to hang the large-format works that they create (paintings of up to 2 x 5 meters). To meet this need, the entrance environment on the north side becomes a gallery. Besides the studio environment, the long building construction is divided into several rooms: on the southwest side are the main bedroom, an office and the toilet, and at the opposite end are the kitchen and the living/dining room. A large chimney separates the kitchen and the dining room from the living area proper.

PHOTOGRAPHS: REINER BLUNCK

North-east elevation

North-west elevation

Site plan

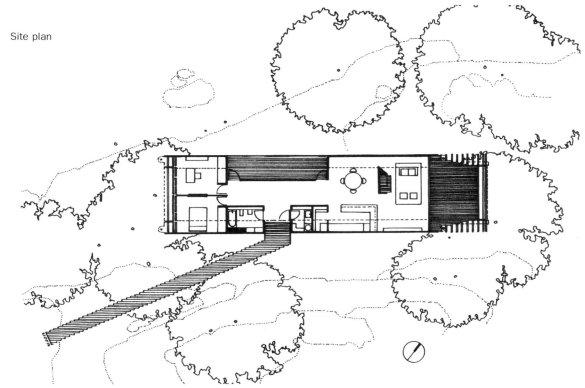

The project combines elements of relation to the environment with a metal sheet wrapping that reinforces its nature as an artificial object.

Two porches, located on the long sides of the volume, extend the surface of the base platform of the construction and help to establish a powerful dialogue with the natural environment.

Large glazed openings and two porches, one at the side and one as a continuation of the base platform, enhance the integration of the building in the environment.

The programme required a space with surfaces on which to hang large paintings that could be used as an exhibition room.

Szyszkowitz + Kowalski
Housing Complex Schießstätte
Graz, Austria

PHOTOGRAPHS: SZYSZKOWITZ + KOWALSKI

The development scheme, with a long curving path cutting through it, was by Heiner Hierzegger, who was commissioned to create an urban design for the site by a housing cooperative. Hierzegger in turn invited several Austrian and foreign architects to carry out different parts of this project. One of these parts, the most important one, was designed by the firm of Szyszkowitz-Kowalski (also responsible for the landscaping of the project).

What Hierzegger intended was to foster a certain diversity joining different forms of expression and characters to create a general impression.

The highly prosaic access area does not follow the general concept. Most of the project, however, meets the desired objectives and the diversity is shown in the sequence of squares and landscaped areas.

The individual sections planned by each group of architects are set along a central path that allows pedestrian access to the complex; while the access to the garages is on the street forming the south boundary.

The public and private open areas take this path as a reference point and unify it in such a way that no details are repeated. The path finishes at the part designed by Szyszkowitz-Kowalski, where it widens into a large courtyard with a double line of trees and fountains that acts as a front courtyard for the last line of apartments and a park for the whole site.

The most outstanding part of the projects of Szyszkowitz-Kowalski is the curved row of buildings lying adjacent a wooded area. This is composed of maisonettes of 50 to 90m² which are accessed from a public path and open staircases. The front gardens are half a level or a whole level above the garage have been built into the hill.

The path leads to an open area in the forest that can be used for meetings or celebrations. The oak trees that rise above the roofs of the dwellings give the final touch to the complex.

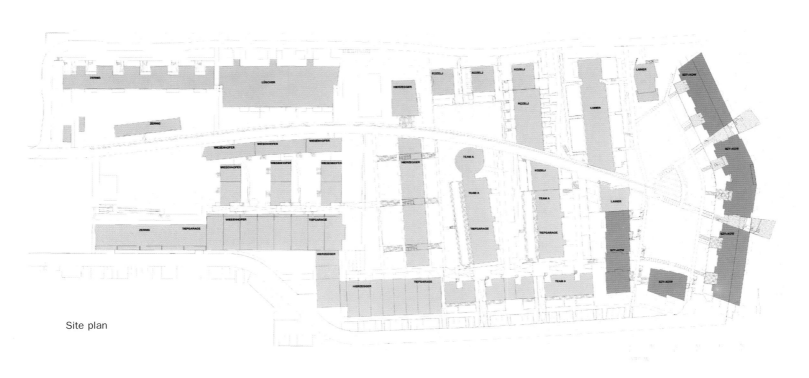

Site plan

One of the criteria of the Szyszkowitz-Kowalski design is certainly consideration of the fact that social diversity and complexity, in the sense of belonging as well as that of territorial relations (above all in the open areas), are formulated within non-specifying frames of reference.

The materials used in the project ensure a minimal environmental impact and allow the building to merge with its surroundings.

Ground floor plan

0   10   20 m

First floor plan

123

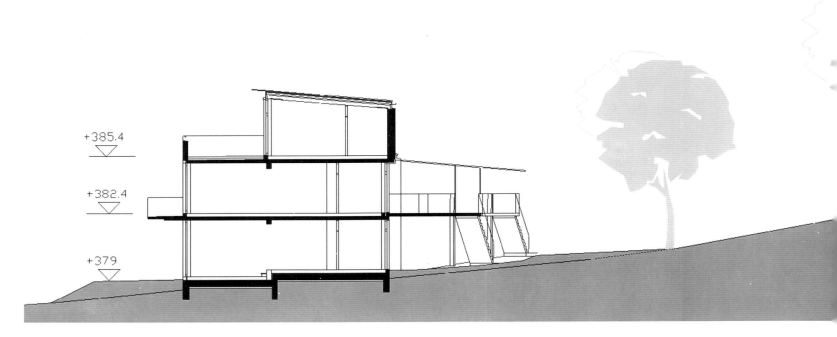

+385.4

+382.4

+379

Cross section

Longitudinal elevation

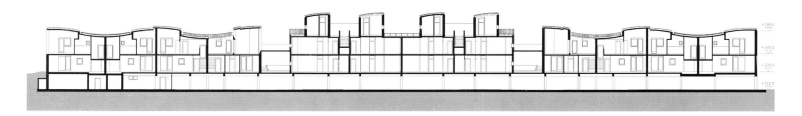

Longitudinal section

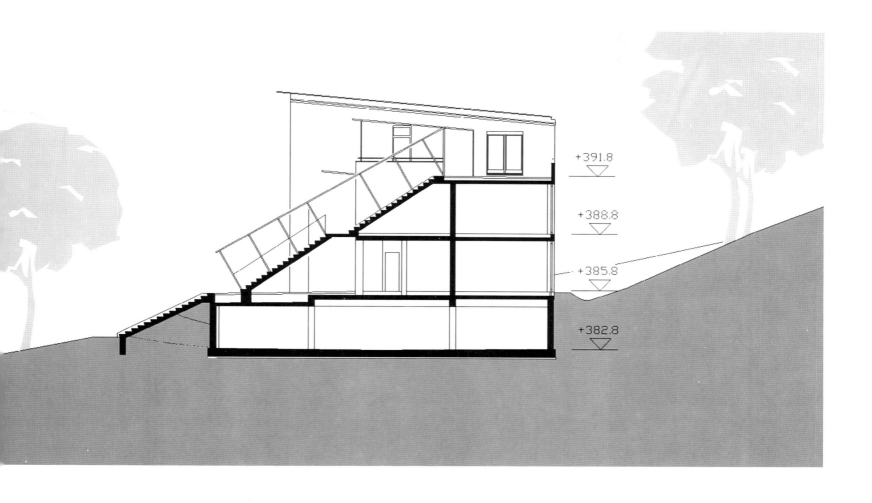

+391.8

+388.8

+385.8

+382.8

The water of a spring runs constantly, rows across the field of waterthroughs and flows alongside the entire lenght of the curved path in an open rivalet.

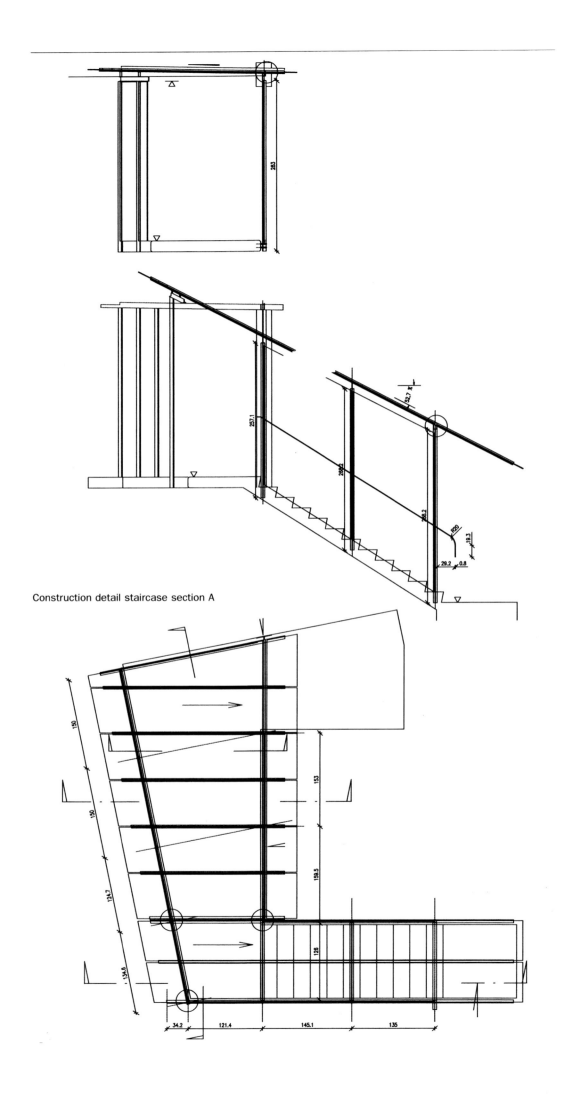

Construction detail staircase section A

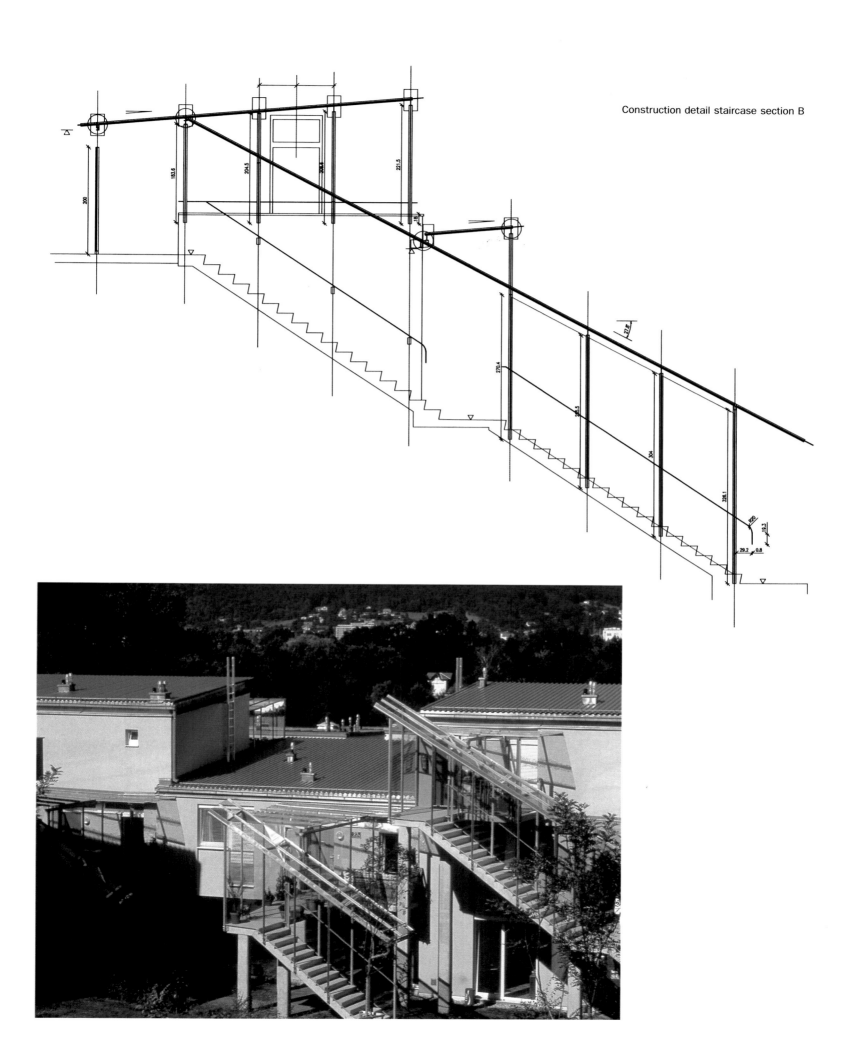

Construction detail staircase section B

Waro Kishi & Associates
House in Higashinada
Kobe, Japan

PHOTOGRAPHS: HIROYUKI HIRAI

This house in Higashinada Ward, Kobe, is for a family of two consisting of a mother and a daughter. The conditions are typical for an urban dwelling. There are houses standing close to the site on both sides, and the site configuration is narrow and quite deep. The saving grace of the project is the presence of a park across the street to the north. The design was started with the idea of "borrowing" the scenery of this park, which penetrates the dwelling through the large glazed openings.

The clients wanted a house in which they could always sense each other's presence. The result is a three-story reinforced concrete house with a continuous interior space.

The concrete box measures 3.3 meters wide and 16 meters deep and occupies nearly the entire site. The south-western quarter of the box has been made into a light well. There is a split-level arrangement between the northern half of the house and the remaining south-eastern quarter, and interior doors have been provided only where necessary.

The living-dining room on the top floor has a ceiling height of 3.9 meters. It faces the light well in the south-western direction, and stairs with low risers lead, beyond the toplit stairwell, to a terrace half a level above the room in the southeastern direction. On the north side, windows are extended the full width of the house and provide the interior spaces with views of the trees and grass in the park across the street. This living-dining room is open to both the north and the south. It floats above the city and enables the occupants to enjoy the townscape. Kishi believes that the only thing an urban dwelling has to offer an occupant is an opportunity to enjoy the city.

Site plan

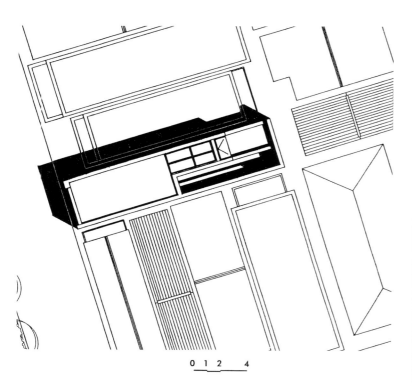

0 1 2 4

The dwelling has views of a park located to the north.

The upper floor, which has a higher ceiling than the rest, thus becomes a semi-open outdoor space.

Third floor plan

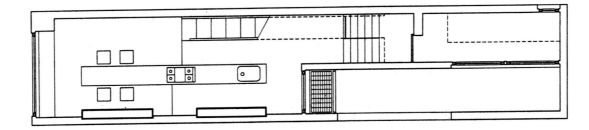

Second floor plan

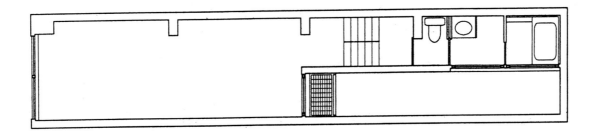

First floor plan

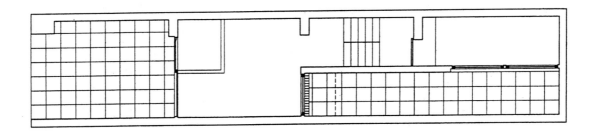

Longitudinal section

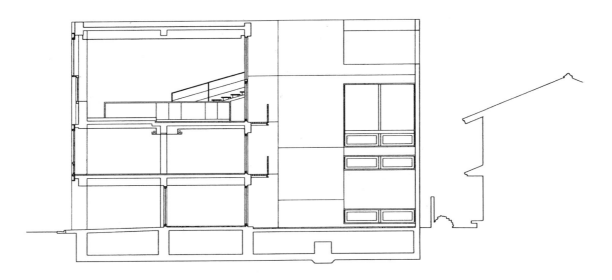

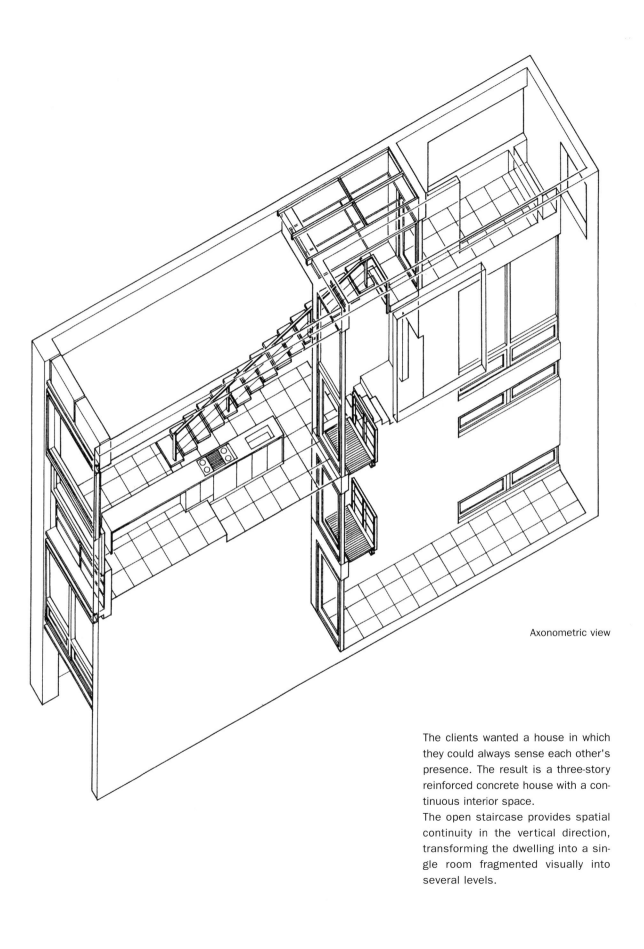

Axonometric view

The clients wanted a house in which they could always sense each other's presence. The result is a three-story reinforced concrete house with a continuous interior space.

The open staircase provides spatial continuity in the vertical direction, transforming the dwelling into a single room fragmented visually into several levels.

Cross-section

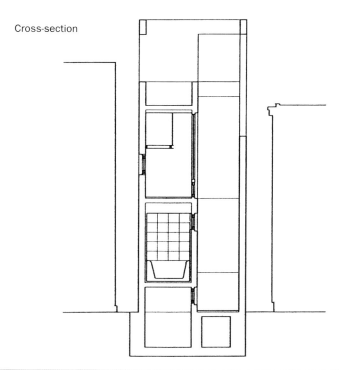

South elevation

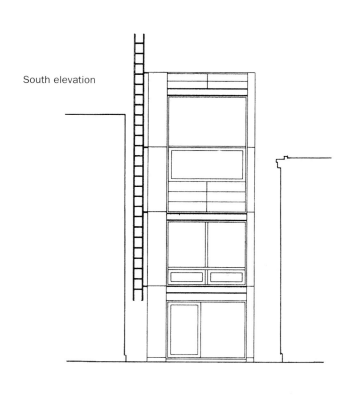

Richard Stacy-Tanner Leddy Maytum Stacy Architects
Corson-Heinser Live/Work
California, USA

The project site was a small vacant lot on a narrow alley in the south of the market district of San Francisco. A gritty industrial landscape characterized by old warehouses and other utilitarian loft structures, this area is slowly evolving into a residential and commercial enclave for artists, designers, start-up businesses and entertainment.

The clients, a designer and a photographer, sought to house their two spaces and their residence in a modern, economical, and adaptable new loft structure. While working within the constraints of the narrow site and their limited budget, they desired maximum volume, openness and natural light in all spaces.

The project is organized on the ground floor, and the graphic design studio opens onto the garden at the rear. The couple's private residence is located on the second level providing a link between the two work studios.

The design of the building is efficiently organized in two parallel zones that extend from front to back. The stair, baths, elevator and storage areas form a narrower zone on the south side. The kitchen and the arrangement of the stacked main stair reinforce this parallel relationship. The building's entrance and a projecting third-floor fire escape are recessed into a vertical slot that marks the internal division between the loft and service spaces. Large in-dustrial sash windows are located at the front and back facades.

The building is supported by concrete piers that extend deep into the mar-shy soil. The piers support a floating concrete platform slab at ground level. Bolted to this base are exposed steel frames designed to resist earthquake forces. The remaining structure of the walls, floors and roof are built of a wood and plywood frame design based on a 4-foot module. Economical and low-maintenance exterior materials (galvanized sheet metal, thin cement board, marine plywood) are assembled into the steel frames. Devoid of decoration and trim, the building's architectural ornament is achieved through the forthright and careful integration of parts, panels and nails. Unpainted, the exterior materials are left to age with time.

On the interior, a similar attitude toward assembly is employed with other in-dustrial materials (opaque acrylic, steel mesh, perforated metal). The trans-parent character of these materials allows natural light to penetrate the vari-ous loft spaces connecting the spaces and diminishing the perception of the narrowness of the building.

PHOTOGRAPHS: THOMAS HEINSER, REINER BLUNCK

Site plan

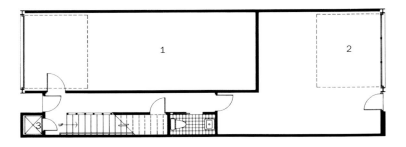

Ground floor plan

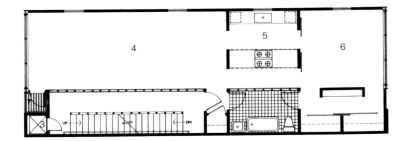

Second floor plan

1. Garage
2. Design studio
3. Dumbwaiter
4. Living room
5. Kitchen
6. Bedroom
7. Balcony
8. Meeting
9. Wardrobe
10. Photography studio
11. Fire escape
12. Dark room
13. Open below
14. Office

The dwelling, located on a narrow site in the South Market district of San Francisco, has a portico structure of exposed steel that is resistant to earthquakes.

While working within the constraints of the narrow site and their limited budget, the clients –a photographer and a graphic designer– desired maximum volume, openness and natural light in all spaces.

The facade was made with materials characteristic of the industrial environment in which the dwelling is located: panels of galvanised metal, wood, exposed concrete and glass.

Third floor plan

Mezzanine

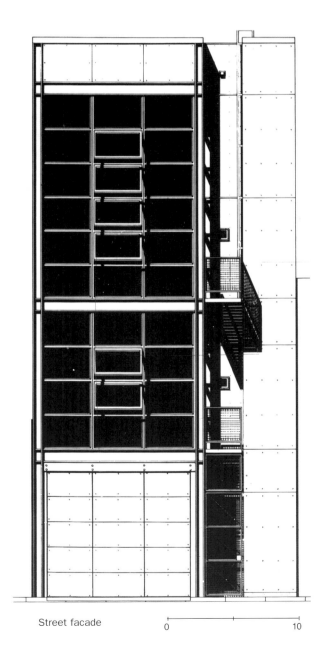

Street facade

0   10

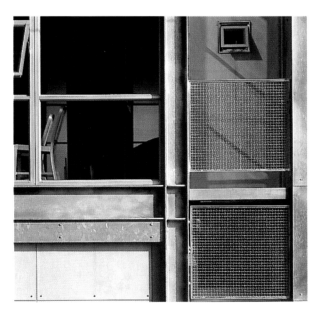

The photographic studio occupies the third floor and the attic to take advantage of the natural light.

The design study located on the ground floor opens onto the rear courtyard.

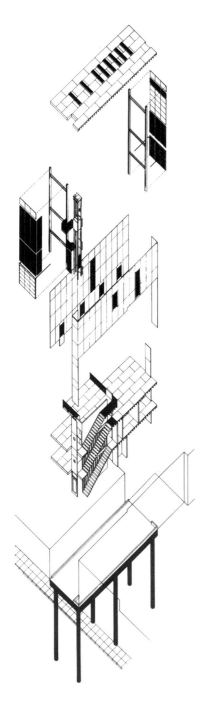

Architectuur Studio Herman Hertzberger
Housing Complex
Düren, Germany

PHOTOGRAPHS: JENS WILLEBRAND

The building, by the studio of the Dutch architect Herman Hertzberger, is located in a rather dismal part of the German town of Düren.

Instead of keeping to the prescribed extension plan and distributing the building blocks all over the site, the project arranges them in a line along the perimeter of the site, thus creating a square building block around a green court in the interior.

This court is accessible from all sides and a street runs through the middle, so that access to the dwellings is through this community space.

The major presence of the continuous roof and the plinth, which shows the difference in building height, provides the whole with a closed and clearly defined form. At the same time, these two elements unify the whole complex.

All dwellings have their entry on the court side and, depending on the housing typology, can be reached directly by stairs or over the different galleries.

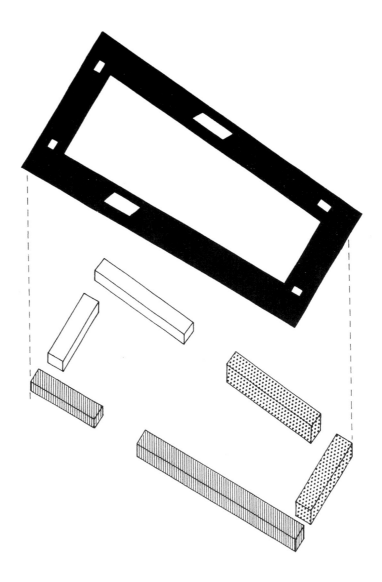

General floor plan

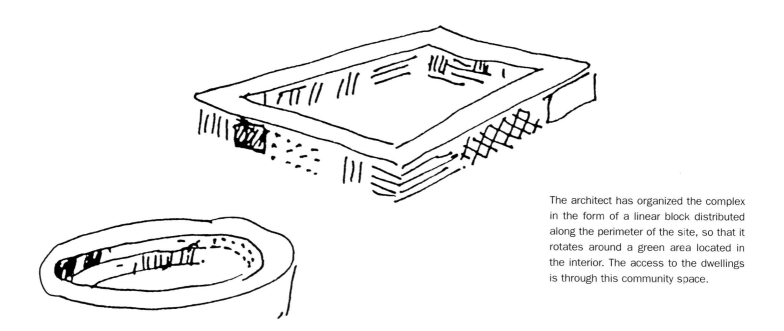

The architect has organized the complex in the form of a linear block distributed along the perimeter of the site, so that it rotates around a green area located in the interior. The access to the dwellings is through this community space.

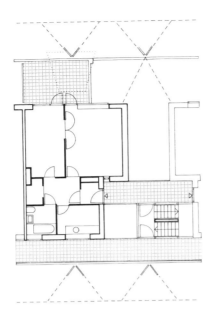

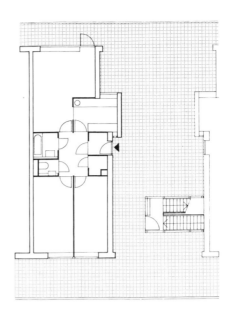

Dwelling Type C. Ground and first floor plan

0   2 m

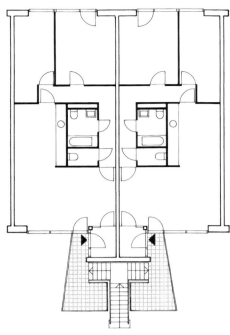

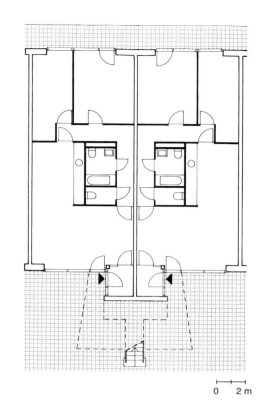

Dwelling Type B. Ground and first floor plan

0   2 m

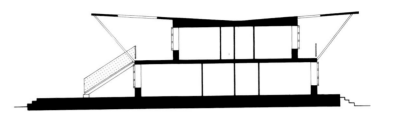

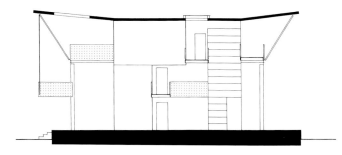

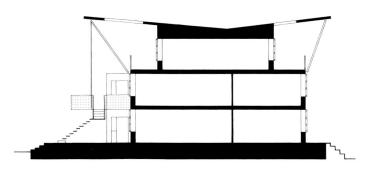

Cross sections of the different housing types

The interior space can be accessed from any of the four streets that define the site by means of open streets under the built building.

The major presence of the continuous roof provides the whole with a closed and clearly defined form. It is thus possible to unify the irregular heights of the units.

Jean Nouvel
Apartments in Tours-Ilot
Tours, France

This city building incorporates some novelties. First, being privately promoted, certain approaches cease to be experimental and come to form part of market demands for housing. Second, the building's mixture of commercial and residential uses, which is the attention paid to its urban implantation.

Unlike the previous projects, in each of which the program is distributed in two longitudinal volumes, this is a single tablet placed parallel to the street. Yet the scheme is essentially the same. Circulation is through an exterior system of metal stairs and ramps attached to the rear facade of the building, and both the dwellings of the top two floors and the offices below are arranged transversally in relation to the narrow bay, an optimal position in terms of ventilation and natural lighting. The double-height ground floor is occupied by the city's Tourist Office as well as by technical premises serving the Convention Center.

With one of its walls painted entirely in Yves Klein's famous blue, the foyer crosses through the building, allowing access to the rear circulation system. The diverse articulations in the floor plan and the section give rise to a wide variety of apartment types within the building, but all have a space between the living room and the street facade, separated by a foldable element. On the top floor, this space becomes a continuous balcony.

The only differentiation made patent on the street-side facade is that between the upper residential body, expressed through a rigorous modular system dominated by the horizontal line, and the commercial-use plinth, formed by vertical glass panels without joineries. Shades that can be rolled up and down at will give a sense of movement to this facade.

PHOTOGRAPHS: JEAN MARIE MONTHIERS

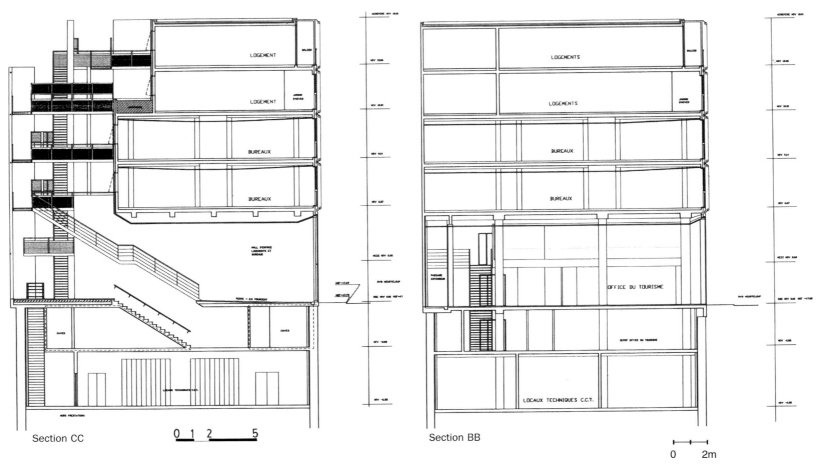

Section CC

0 1 2 5

Section BB

0   2m

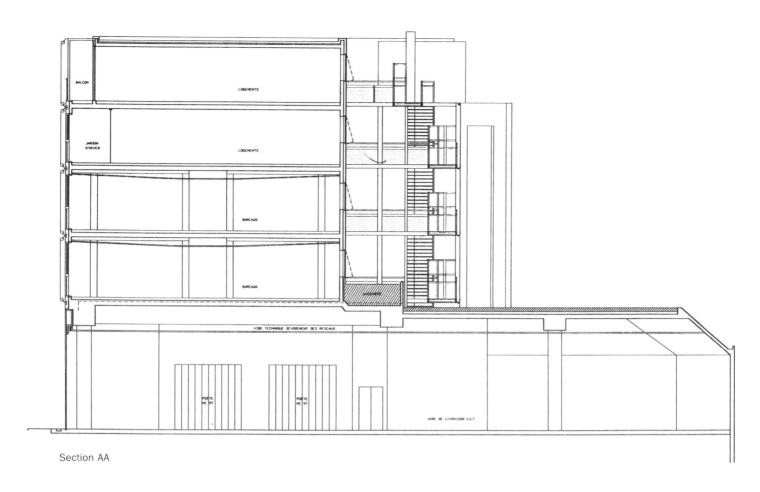

Section AA

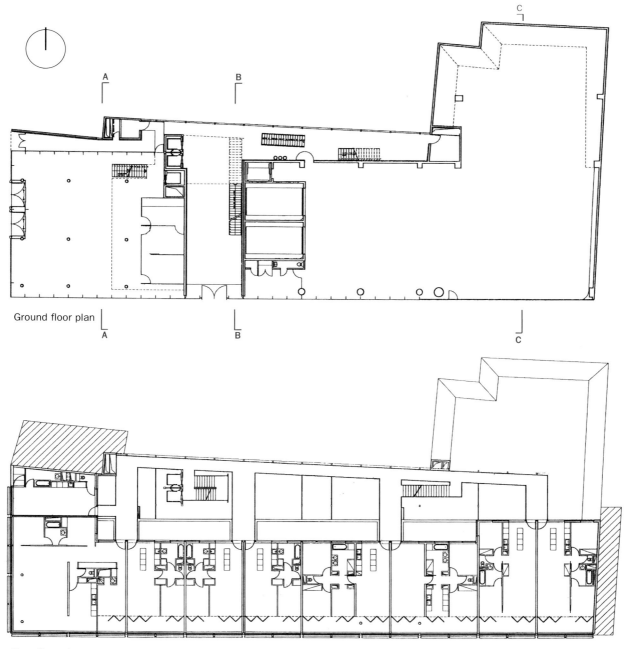

Ground floor plan

Type floor plan

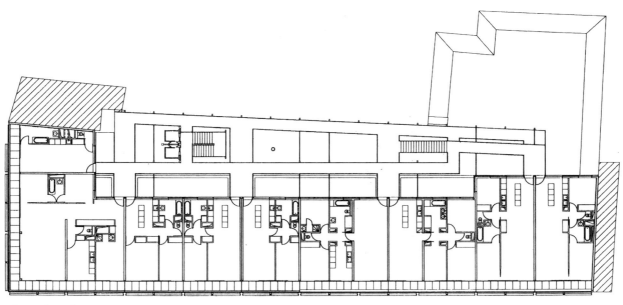

Upper floor plan

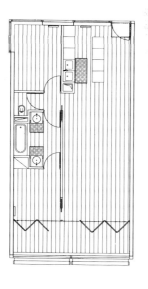

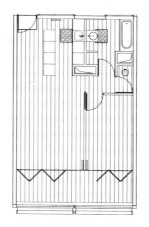

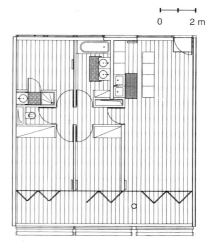

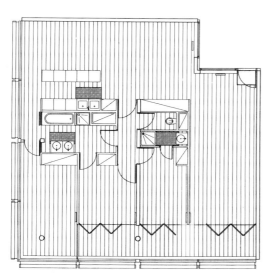

Dwelling Type floor plans

View of the entrance hall, with one of the walls painted entirely in Yves Klein blue.

COOP HIMMELB(L)AU
SEG Apartment Tower
Vienna, Austria

This 60m high tower, in conjunction with two other projected high rise buildings, forms the new district known as "Donau City". It includes 70 apartments, 9 eating facilities and offices on 25 floors.

Two major considerations were important in the design of the outer form of the building. On the one hand, the concept of the tower is based on the idea of putting two houses, one on top of the other, in a way such that a common space would occur at the intersection. This common space –called a sky lobby– is then used for the accommodation of a venue, a playground, a "teleworking café" and a sundeck. On the other hand, the concept of the so called climate facade was developed, which both links and surrounds the two components.

This is an "intelligent" glass facade that, along with the "air box" on top of the roof and the circulation core (planned as a heat accumulator), regulates the cooling of the apartments in summer and the heating in winter. This well calculated system offers a higher level of comfort during hot weather and a minimizing of costs during the heating period. Besides its function as a sound buffer, the climate facade provides space for glazed loggias placed in front of the apartments. These loggias allow green spaces, an element not normally seen in high rise buildings, and open views of the city and natural surroundings, also uncommon for urban living.

All apartments (ranging from 55m² to 130m²) are based on a loft concept with an open plan without load-bearing walls. This concept enables a flexible layout of all the apartments.

The concept of the glass skin surrounding the building enables an orientation of all buildings towards the south. The glass facade, developed from the architectural concept, is intended to passively exploit solar energy. Using wind energy to power engines will further provide the necessary air circulation.

PHOTOGRAPHS: ANNA BLAU, GERALD ZUGMANN

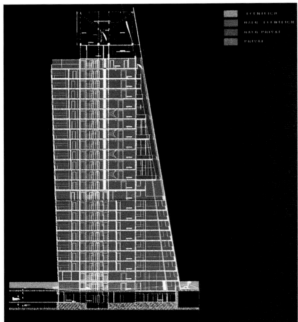

The glass facade, which faces southeast and southwest, is the medium through which thermal energy is stored as radiant energy potential during the winter, spring and autumn. The thermal energy produced during daylight hours is supplied to a thermal reservoir unit located in the interior of the building.

CA CB   CC CD   CE

Twenty-first floor plan

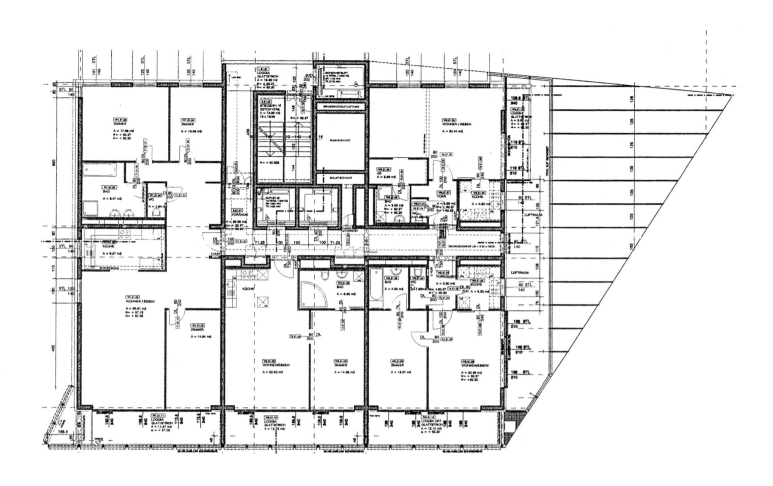

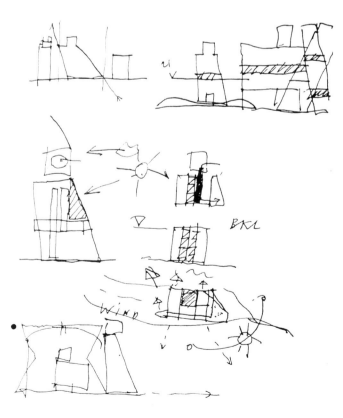

Section AA

The central thermal mass is a reinforced concrete shaft, which is equipped with heat exchange surfaces. To guarantee exchange between the loggia and the climate facade, air circulation between the two systems is provided mechanically. This air circulation is affected by the ventilators in the thermal mass shaft.

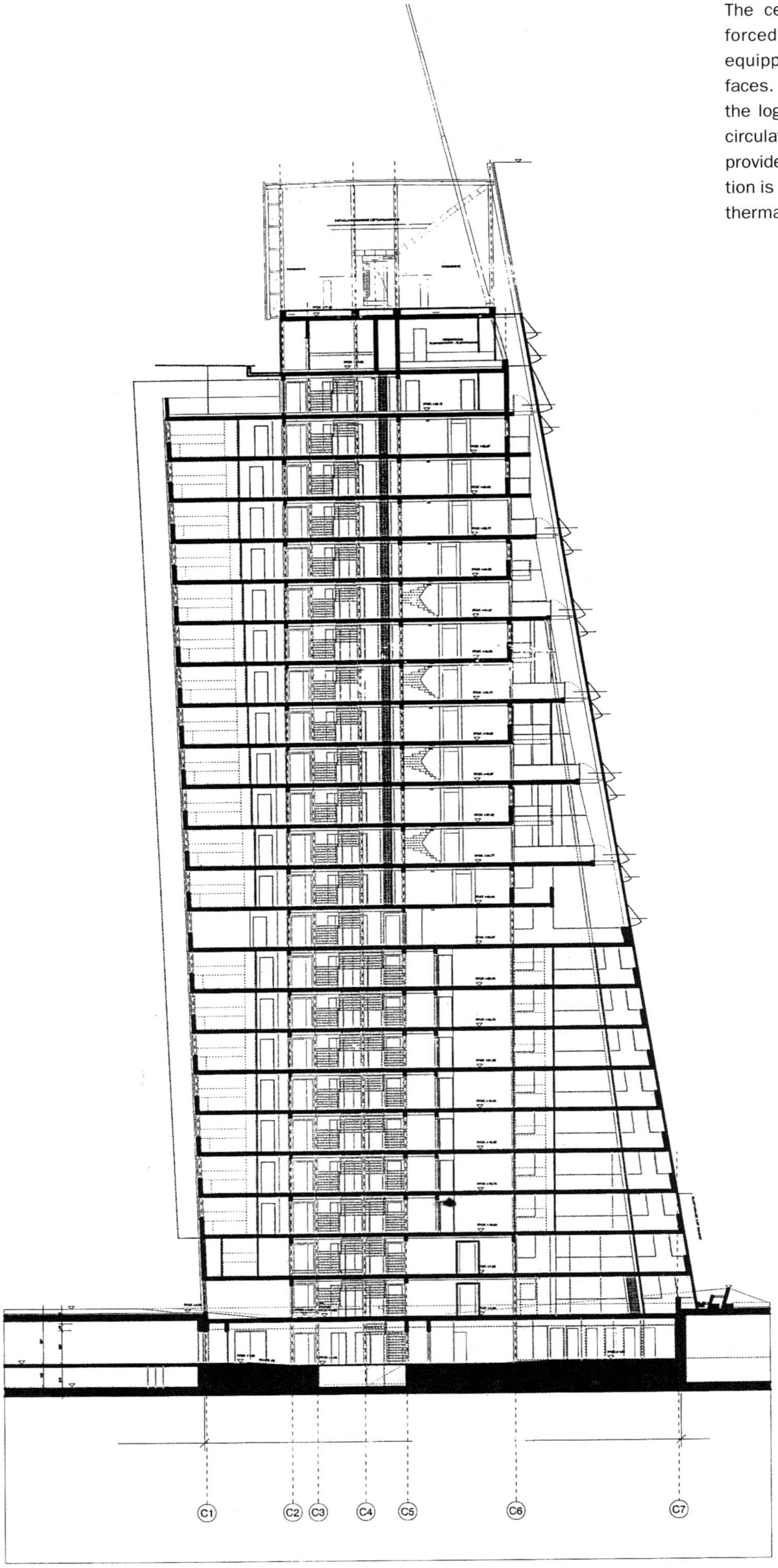

C1 C2 C3 C4 C5 C6 C7

Skylobby, ninth floor plan

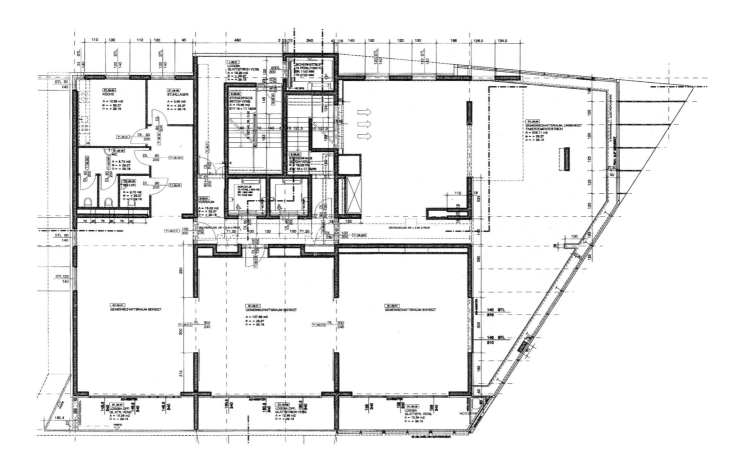

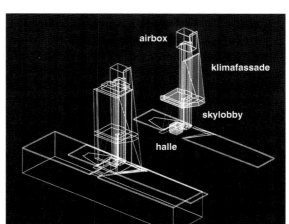

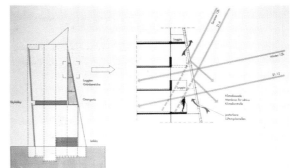

First floor plan

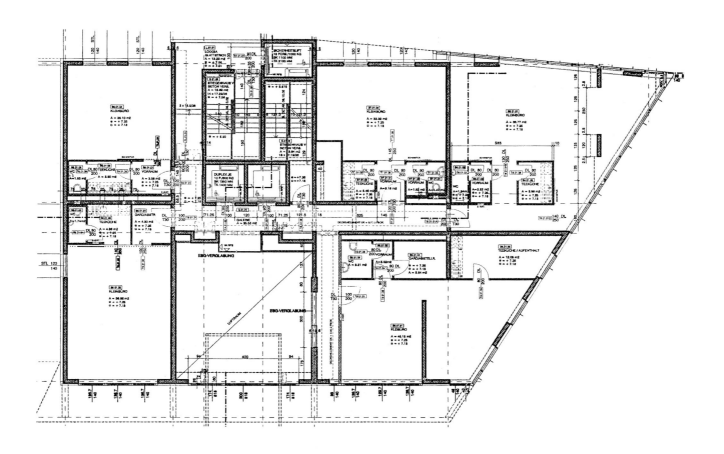

Shoei Yoh + Architects
Sundial Welfare Facility for Seniors
Fukuoka, Japan

This is a welfare facility designed to accommodate senior citizens who need help with physical or mental problems and to help them maintain a certain level of independence.

The architecture itself was conceived as an urban space in which, through social activities shared with acquaintances, the self support potential of the inhabitants will be given incentive.

Two rectangular wings meeting at an angle of 112.5° produce a fan-shaped atrium in between. The atrium, covered with layers of transparent and wired glass, is a semi-outdoor space for rehabilitation and recreation where one can feel the moderate changes of natural light and wind; this also serves as a stage in which performances such as concerts, plays and dances can take place.

PHOTOGRAPHS: SHOEI YOH

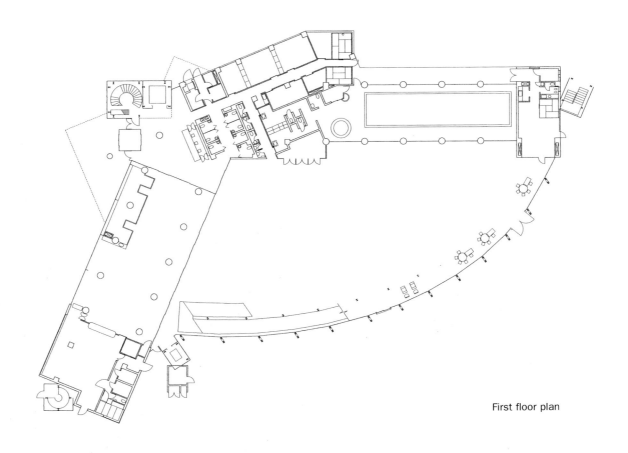

First floor plan

0 1 2 4

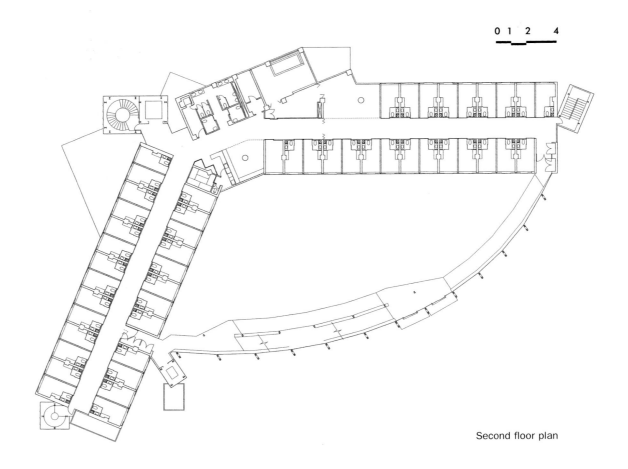

Second floor plan

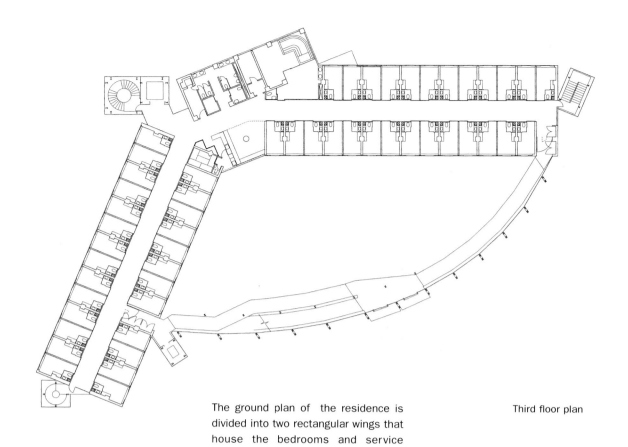

Third floor plan

The ground plan of the residence is divided into two rectangular wings that house the bedrooms and service areas, and an atrium that occupies the corner between the two wings and is used for sundry activities.

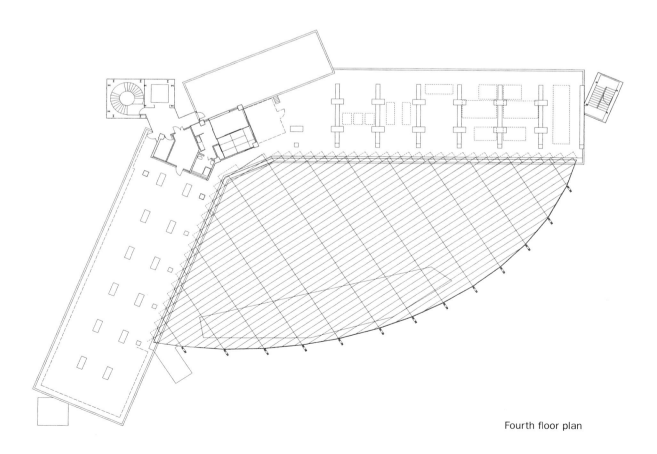

Fourth floor plan

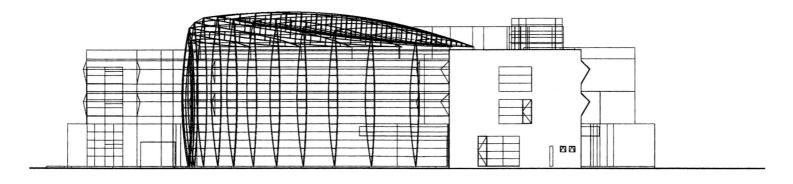

East elevation

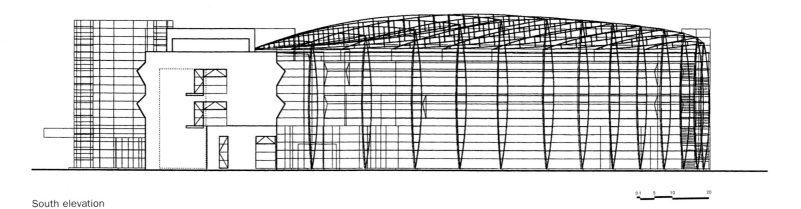

South elevation

The architect created a large atrium flooded with light by means of the massive use of glass in the curved wall of the south facade and the roof.

The great transparency of the facade of Sundial House II provides a constant relationship with the surroundings from the interior of a closed space.

From the structural point of view, all the glass walls were designed to withstand wind and snowfall.

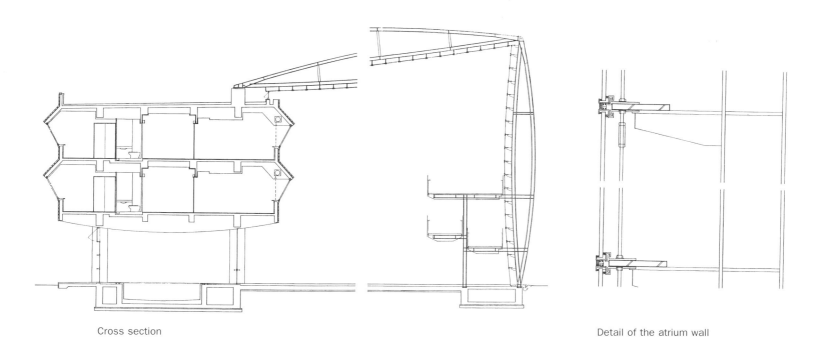

Cross section

Detail of the atrium wall